You Got an Ology?

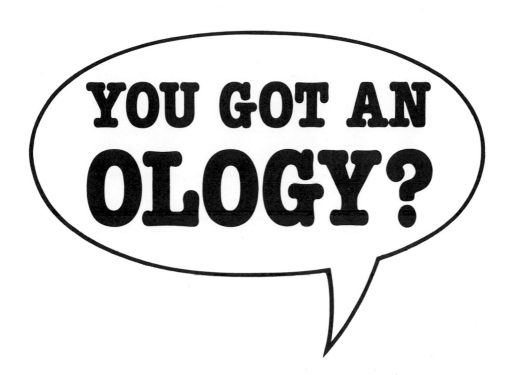

YOU GOT AN OLOGY?

MAUREEN LIPMAN
& RICHARD PHILLIPS

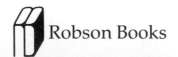
Robson Books

The publishers would like to thank
British Telecom for their co-operation.

First published in Great Britain in 1989 by Robson Books Ltd,
Bolsover House, 5–6 Clipstone Street, London W1P 7EB

Copyright © 1989 Original scripts British Telecom, additional
material Maureen Lipman and Richard Phillips

British Library Cataloguing in Publication Data
Lipman, Maureen,
   You got an ology?
   1. Great Britain. Television advertising
   I. Title II. Phillips, Richard
   659.14'3'0941

ISBN 0 86051 598 2

Typeset by Bookworm Typesetting, Manchester
Printed in Great Britain by Butler & Tanner Ltd, Frome and London

ACKNOWLEDGEMENTS

Special thanks to: Ollie Ball for all his photographs, Complete Video, Nigel Foster, Claire Haffenden, Moving Picture Company, Derek Sternberg, Linda Wade, who designed the book, and Louise Dixon (our dynamic editor without whom, forget it).

Thanks also to the splendid cast, especially: Christina Avery, Sarah Beagley, Elizabeth Bennett, Janie Booth, Bernard Bresslaw, Vincent Brimble, Mike Burns, Sandra Caron, Geoffrey Chiswick, Brian Greene, Linal Haft, Alistair Kent, Jacob Krichefski, Miriam Margolyes, Zia Mohyeddin, Hayley Napper, Kate Orton, Richard Platt, Simon Prebble, Caroline Quentin, Ian Target, Lee Walker and Richard Wilson.

From the production side: Gerald Berman, Adrian Biddle, Alex Booker, Malcolm Bristow, Berry Bronkhurst, Bob Brooks, Francine Brown, Roger Burridge, John Cigarini, Caroline Cobbold, Eddie Collins, Steve Cook, Frazer Copp, Nick Diss, Dave Fordham, Geoff Forster, Steve Gandolfi, Lilliana Gibbs, Roger Hall, Simon Holland, Adrian Hughes, Wanda Kelly, Matthew Longfellow, Lorna Magowan, Phil Meheux, Louis Muslin, Daphne Paris, Roy Rodhouse, Rob Rowan, Mostyn Rowlands, Nick Saward, Paul Sharkey, Tony Smith, Nick Swingler, Ken Tuohy, Ian Weil, Ken Wesbury, Jean Winter.

From J Walter Thompson: Lisa Bamber, Peter Celiz, Paul Chown, Dave Cockburn, Alison Cummins, Joanna Dickerson, Amanda Goodship, Christine Grey, Mike Hall, Gary Heffernan, David Millar, Lynda Morgan, Ted O'Brien, Richard Saunders, Allen Thomas and Bill Wallace.

And, last but not least, from British Telecom: Karen Austin, Mark Baker, Mike Bowtell, David Butcher, Caroline Chamberlain, Tim Evans, Katrina Fargie, Chris Fry, Les Harris, Adrian Hosford, Duncan Ingram, Nick Kane, Tim McKay, Sheila Mitchell, Phil Mounsey, Paul Reynolds, Howard Sandom, Edward Scott, Ray Smith, Jan Rexwinkel, John Turner, John Varley, and Tony Wren.

And extra special thanks from Richard to Chrissie who has had to live through it all; and from Maureen to Jack, for reasons they'll never know.

For Zelma Lipman,
the late Ena Phillips,
and everybody else's mother too!

WHAT MAKES BEATTIE RUN

by RICHARD PHILLIPS

In the fifties, an American by the ultimate fifties-American name of Vance Packard, wrote a book about advertising called *The Hidden Persuaders*. It was an influential book. Or at least its name was. *The Hidden Persuaders* perfectly summed up what people thought advertising was all about. It suggested an image of advertising as being a mysterious world full of shadowy Svengalis, fiendish manipulators who knew precisely how to bend the public to their will.

Naturally, people in the advertising business lapped it up. Jolly flattering to be regarded as being so diabolically clever. And rather profitable. For diabolical cleverness is, of course, what advertisers pay big bucks for.

Ah, but if only it were true. If only we did have some special insight into the sub-conscious; if only the subtle, hidden meanings that so-called experts are forever finding in advertising, were actually there. In my experience, the truth is very different. The most vital ingredient for the concoction of any successful piece of advertising is a large slice of luck. The British Telecom campaign is a case in point.

It all began when one of my fellow copywriters at J Walter Thompson – the advertising agency at which I work – went on holiday. At the time there was a Telecom campaign running which featured various furry animals, but the decision had been taken to put it down. This other chap, in partnership with an art director, had been asked to think of something new. (Using a 'copywriter/art director team' is the standard way of doing things in advertising agencies.)

It seemed that all the hard work had been done. They had come up with a basic idea for which four commercials were needed initially, and by the time he went on holiday they had thought of three. So all I was brought in to do was help the art director think of the fourth.

The first thing, of course, was to see what they had already done. Unfortunately (or perhaps fortunately as it turned out) I didn't much like what I saw. However, the art director, Joanna Dickerson, happened to be an old friend of mine, so I was able to summon up the courage to tell her. As it turned out she wasn't too struck on them either, so we started afresh.

Now, before one is asked to think of an ad, one is given what is called a 'brief'. And this 'brief' explains precisely what the client wants to say about whatever it is they are planning to advertise. So, having chucked everything into the waste-paper bin, we went back to the 'brief'. Or rather 'briefs', because there were lots of different points they wanted to make. And this is where fate showed its hand. The first piece of paper I picked up told me that they wanted 'to encourage people to understand the value of a phone call in an inter-family relationship'. And then came the bit I understood: 'e.g. Phone your mother'.

Here I was, a nice Jewish boy of nearly 40 years experience, being asked to write a commercial about phoning your mother. Talk about the right man for the job! Without question, I was one of the world's greatest living authorities on the subject of phoning your mother. Given all this, it was but a miniscule leap for me to think of using the character of a Jewish mother in a commercial. The mother who treats a telephone line as the next best thing to an umbilical cord is a familiar character in Jewish humour. For a Jewish copywriter faced with such a brief, putting her into a commercial was the obvious thing to do.

So I wrote a script in which a Jewish mother complains her son never calls; then, when he does call, she complains that he can only call, he can never visit. I showed it to Joanna. At this stage I had two serious doubts about the idea, and one was that you would have to be Jewish to find it funny. But Joanna (who isn't Jewish) was certain it would work.

So I picked up the rest of the briefs to see if there was more than one commercial in this idea. They wanted a commercial to get people to use the phone as an aid to shopping; I wrote the Mrs Jones commercial. They wanted a commercial to persuade people to use the phone for birthday greetings; I wrote the 'voice like an angel' commercial. And they used the greetings card as a model for another brief: phone to say congratulations. I wrote the 'ology' commercial. It certainly seemed as though the idea was campaignable.

But I wasn't keen to progress it until I was certain that my second doubt was unfounded. This concerned a more sensitive area. Would Jewish people be offended by seeing a Jewish character portrayed in a commercial? On the one hand I could see' no reason why they should be. Being Jewish myself, I was obviously going to make sure we would paint an affectionate portrait, and I saw nothing in the scripts that would cause any trouble. On the other hand, you tend to be very partisan about scripts you have written yourself. So I asked around amongst Jewish people I knew. In particular I asked my brother. Though the character was certainly not consciously based on my own mother (she would have been horrified to think she was remotely like her), I thought my brother would be the first to take offence. He didn't. And neither did anybody else I asked.

I didn't take this to mean that I would please everybody (two Jews, three opinions, as they say) but I was reasonably satisfied I wasn't going to cause serious offence. In fact, when the commercials started to run there was quite a lot of correspondence in the *Jewish Chronicle*; the balance of which, I was relieved to see, was favourable.

With my doubts assuaged, I felt ready to show the scripts inside the agency. This bit of the advertising process can often lead to some fairly serious verbal abuse, but in this case everyone seemed to like what they saw, so there was no need to round on anyone and make the usual accusations of philistinism. (Pity really, it would have been rather nice to have called somebody a Philistine in this context.)

Now came the tricky bit. Flogging the idea to the client. That is to say, I *assumed* it would be the tricky bit, because it invariably is. Big organizations rarely have one person to make yes or no decisions on the spot. They are usually composed of endless layers of management each of which has to give its stamp of approval. And within these layers there can be committees, and within these committees there can be factions. And within these factions there are always arses, which must at all times be covered. In other words, the infant mortality rate for advertising ideas is very high indeed. It wouldn't be so bad, if it were survival of the fittest but of course it isn't; when any committee decision is involved it's survival of the least controversial.

The curious thing about British Telecom is that despite its size it utterly failed to fulfil my expectations of the worst. Yes, we did have to present the ideas to lots of people, but I kept on coming across individuals who actually had an opinion and were prepared to give it without waiting for their boss to speak first. Perhaps I'm a bit biased because most of their opinions were favourable, but I found British Telecom extraordinarily flexible and responsive for a big company. All the key people – Adrian Hosford, Howard Sandom, David Butcher, Tim Evans, Les Harris, Ray Smith, Duncan Ingram – were actually prepared to make a decision and commit themselves to it. And the decision they wanted to make was to make the commercials.

However there was a proviso. And that proviso was that the campaign would have to face the hurdle of market research. In other words, a research company would be hired to go out and ask members of the general public – the target market, as it is called in adspeak – what they thought of the idea. Had they asked for anything less, I would not have been merely surprised, I would have been thunderstruck. Even the most gung-ho clients like their judgement supported by research. I can't say I blame them. Indeed, in principle, I absolutely agree with them. Just as I had wanted to find out if the campaign might cause offence amongst the Jewish community, so the client wanted to check out whether it would actually work. The trouble is that principles are one thing, and practise quite another.

Like 99.99 per cent of all advertising 'creatives' I dread research. It seems to work on the plague of locusts principle: one minute you think you've got something and then nibble, nibble, nibble and there's nothing left at all. Don't ask me why this should be. It just is. There doesn't seem to be any method of researching advertising which doesn't put the unorthodox idea – that is to say the idea that hasn't been seen a thousand times before – in dire peril.

So Dora (as Beattie was called before she was called Beattie) was to be exposed to research. The question was, in what form? We didn't have the films to show – the whole point of the research was to find out if they were worth making. We thought about and rejected the idea of using something called an 'animatic', which is like a rather rough cartoon. In the end we opted for the 'narrative tape', a sound-only format that works a bit like a radio commercial.

Not that our narrative tapes did any of the ideas much justice. At this early stage, no-one had thought of asking Maureen to play the part, so we didn't even have what has now become the authentic Dora/Beattie voice. In fact, we tried several well known actresses, all of whom are usually tremendously funny, but we just weren't able to bring the ideas to life. Tough really. Because time, tide and market research waits for no man. We had to give them something, so we gave them what we had. I fully expected Dora, Melvyn, Anthony, Mrs Jones et al to disappear straight down the pan.

This time my expectations of the worst were not only fulfilled, they were utterly eclipsed. The research results turned out to be unimaginably awful. To cut a long story short, it seemed that no-one liked anything. It was the researcher's view that if the campaign was to have any chance of success, the central character would have to reflect a much more contemporary lifestyle. She would have to become, in an immortal phrase, a 'tracksuit granny'. 'A what?' we chorused, and with this question tapped an almost bottomless well of pseudo-sociological gobbledygook about 'the eighties woman', the main point of which was, as I recall, that she liked to go jogging or do aerobics. Quite what this had to do with anything I had no idea. But it was clear to me that unless every member of the assembled party suddenly fell prey to an attack of collective amnesia, this campaign was, as they say, dead in the water. (Even before it went down the pan.)

It was at this point that something remarkable happened. I won't say it was a miracle, but divine intervention can't be ruled out. The corpse began to revive.

I was about halfway through a pointless last minute effort to lock the stable door after the horse has not only bolted but signed up for a five year stint with the French Foreign Legion – that is to say I was bitterly complaining about every dot and comma of the research – when it dawned on me I was not alone: Our clients were not yet ready to pronounce the idea dead. Over the next few days they came to the conclusion that they wanted to discount this research. They believed that the narrative tapes had been inadequate, and that if the idea was to be properly sounded out, we had to bite the bullet and make the films. Only with proper actors, performances and sets could the campaign be judged.

Having received this completely unexpected green light we had to set about making the commercials. I shall skip over most of this process – if only because there was so many dramas and disasters it would take a lot more space than I have here to do the story any kind of justice – except for one vital moment: the moment when it first dawned on me that Maureen Lipman might be the person we were looking for. The blindingly obvious registered at last. Here was the person with exactly the right combination of qualities – an acerbic wit but a natural charm – that would be right for the overbearing, but nevertheless lovable, character we wanted to create. So what if she was about thirty years younger than the old girl we had in mind? What was make-up for, if not to lie about a lady's age?

So, some weeks later, complete with Ms Lipman in the part, we took ten completed films back to the client. (New 'briefs' had proliferated in the meantime and, therefore, scripts and films as well.) The big question was: Did they work? Now that we had had full benefit of cast, lights, camera, action, did we have a winner? Or as the research had predicted were we in receipt of the most celebrated turkey since the Cratchets got theirs?

When we first showed the commercials they got a generally warm response. I won't say they were greeted with uproarious laughter, but most people inside the agency and British Telecom seemed quite happy with the results. Of course this was not conclusive. There was still the great god Research to please. So off went the campaign to be researched once again, and a couple of weeks later we all met to hear what the researcher had to say. And guess what? The results apparently, were every bit as bad as they had been the first time. I responded predictably. I scoffed. I screamed. I swore. I might as well have saved my breath, because, once again, the angels were on my side. They alighted on the shoulders of all the clients present and whispered in their ears: could these commercials really be as bad as all that? Could their own personal, spontaneous reaction be so at odds with the general public's? Could there not, instead, be something wrong with this research?

And that's how it all happened. As I recall, there wasn't even a very prolonged discussion. They quickly made up their minds that crummy research or no, the campaign was good enough to run. It was a triumph of personal judgement over a welter of so-called statistical evidence. In the circumstances, it was a remarkably gutsy decision. But it was a decision that was quickly vindicated. Almost immediately the campaign started running, it was getting press attention. I think Anne Robinson of the *Daily Mirror* was the first journalist to write about it. It was the 'ology' line that caught her imagination and she wasn't alone. It was this commercial that gave the campaign its momentum. For me, as the writer, this was particularly gratifying. To find a line that one has written border on becoming a national catchphrase gives the old ego a hell of a boost. And what the *Mirror* began, Wapping soon took up. We were in *The Times*, we were in the *Sun* ('Twenty things you didn't know about your favourite Jewish momma.' What else?)

Soon it became time for the annual round of advertising awards. The advertising industry, which is every bit as keen on awards as the film or music industries, seems to be handing out one kind of meritricious gong or another every week of the year. Still, it's always nice to win, so we were very happy when, in no time at all, we found tasteless perspex and brass thingummies of every shape and size raining down upon us. Of course, there was the occasional brickbat to go with the bouquets, and not all the commercials did as well as each other. Of the original ten films, three have never run. And another, about an answering machine, which happens to be one of Maureen's particular favourites despite being the only film in the series in which she does not appear, ran only a couple of times.

By the time we came to our second major 'shoot', we'd learned some important lessons. The first was that making ten films in one go was far too many, so we attempted only four. One of these was 'Do you have a 12 in the Green?' the commercial in which our heroine drives Mr Edwin, the local Hardy Amies, to distraction, as she interrogates him about the availability of every size and colour in the shop. This commercial, which featured the superbly apopleptic Richard Wilson as Mr Edwin, and indeed every one of the eighteen that were made before the end of 1988, was ingeniously directed by Tony Smith, the man who made the BAFTA award-winning BBC series *Tutti Frutti*.

It was during this shoot that Dora finally metamorphosed into Beattie. A clever pun that came from Maureen, and which we seized upon immediately. Even if it hadn't been such a nifty play on BT, it would still have been just the right kind of name for our character. As it was, it was perfect.

At about this time, I decided – or maybe someone decided for me – that I needed a break from British Telecom. But while I went off to slog away on other campaigns, the Beattie show went on. Other writers and art directors from JWT, Richard Saunders, Peter Celiz and Paul Chown were given the always difficult task of seamlessly continuing a campaign that was already up and running, and three more films were made.

At the beginning of 1989 there were several new developments. Firstly, we – that is J Walter Thompson and Beattie – were asked to advertise British Telecom's international calls as well as the domestic service and I came back to write these scripts. (Whereupon I found our new clients from the international division, Edward Scott, John Varley, and Paul Reynolds, to be every bit as positive as the others had been.)

Secondly, Tony Smith, who had done so much to set the style of the campaign, was involved in directing a feature film, so we had to look for a new director. Thirdly, Joanna, who hadn't really been involved since the first shoot, returned to the team, but this time working with Linda Morgan on some new domestic scripts.

Joanna's contribution to the world of Beattie has been absolutely vital. Because it was my natural milieu, and because she had the sense to recognize this, she took the decision at the beginning to stand back and let me get on with it. But it's never easy for a 'creative' person to be so self-effacing. We always want our ideas to be the ones that carry the day. It's a tribute to Joanna's remarkable maturity and lack of ego that she was prepared to give me *carte blanche*. She never lost her enthusiasm though, and without her support, and particularly her initial instinct that this campaign idea really would work, I am absolutely certain that Beattie would never have got off the ground.

In looking for a new director, Joanna and Linda chose Bob Brooks, who had directed the George Cole and David Bailey films for Olympus. He also agreed to shoot one of the international commercials I had written, in which Beattie calls her younger brother Lionel in Toronto. Or rather not in Toronto because we actually never went further than a studio in Wembley.

But for the two Australian scripts, which featured Maureen playing Beattie's Sydney-based sister Rose, we really had to be down under. There were exterior shots that couldn't be convincingly faked. For these two films, I chose yet another director. Me. So it was that in April 1989 we went off to Sydney, where I had the time of my life shouting 'Action' and 'Cut'. And having once got my teeth into the director's megaphone, I wasn't about to give it up. Mixing a metaphor, I've got myself back into harness as writer too, and as I write this we have just completed the two latest films in the series, numbers 25 and 26. One of these features two new characters, Beattie's good friends, Dolly and Gerald, played by the splendid Miriam Margolyes and Bernard Bresslaw.

In fact, all the actors who have appeared in the series, have, without exception, been splendid. Some, of course, have had bigger parts than others: Jacob Krichefski as the unscholarly grandson Anthony, Linel Haft as the long suffering son Melvyn, and Geoffrey Chiswick, magnificently stoic as the even longer suffering husband Harry.

There have been stars in the background too. To name just a few: Vi Shilling, the costume designer; Eddie Collins, the camera operator; Roger Hall and Roger Burridge, set designers; Gerald Berman and Adrian Hughes, production company producers; Mostyn Rowlands, lighting cameraman; and Nigel Foster, J Walter Thompson's producer (and my minder!). And last but not least there is Ian Weil, editor extraordinaire, whose fine touch with the scissors has, twenty times or more, managed to condense the best of what we had into a minute or less.

Did I say last but not least? I almost forgot Maureen, without whom we would most certainly not be where we are today. It is quite simply impossible to imagine anyone else playing the part. Her contribution has been incalculable.

Talking of contributions here's a rough guide to who has done what in this book. The scripts, of which we have reproduced twenty (including, as a matter of interest, a couple that have never run), are almost exactly as they were originally scripted and performed. It's a measure of Maureen's ability as an actress that she makes the lines seem her own, but although she often spontaneously adds on brilliant little bits to the end of a script – like the 'it's the teachers I blame' line in the 'ology' commercial – she is, by and large, very faithful to the words that I and the other writers have actually put down. Other than that, she has written just about everything in this book and apart from turning up at the odd editorial meeting, I have done little more than be the head cook and bottlewasher. Amongst other things, Maureen has added a completely new dimension to the original scripts – all of Beattie's unspoken thoughts.

Somehow though, I don't think you can see the joins. There seems to be a bit of Beattie in both of us. In fact, I tend to think there's a bit of Beattie in all of us. And that, if anything, is the secret of her success.

HELLO, HELLO

from Maureen Lipman

I suppose the first time I became aware that Beattie was bigger than both of us was one Saturday in February 1989 just after a visit to a Vietnamese acupuncturist. I would put the time at 1.20, the location Baker Street and my companion a clone-like version of myself, my daughter Amy, fresh as a daisy after having a needle in her skull and combing the newsagent's windows for a magazine with Kylie Minoguery in it. Please! Find me a magazine *without* Kylie Minoguery in it. Suddenly Amy stopped dead in her tracks and said 'Mod – what does THAT mean?' 'THAT' turned out to be the headlines in bold black type, of an advertising magazine called *Campaign* and the headline concerned read:

LIPMAN SET TO TAKE OVER THE WORLD.

It was the turn of my tracks to be stopped dead in. I swallowed, with difficulty. It could mean one of three things:

1) My brother, who is in the airline business, had made a takeover bid for PAN-AM.
2) I had unwittingly lent my name to some obscure army of liberation under the misapprehension that it was a ladies' luncheon club in Brent.
3) I was still fast asleep with a needle in my skull and dreaming of Broadway.

But, two of us had seen the sinister sentence and two of us now approached it with stealth. A short and shifty read explained what had been clear to J Walter Thompson's advertising company and British Telecom for some time. Out of the five advertising agencies covering various aspects of BT's current campaign, one of them, JWT, had beaten off another to win the International Phone Calls contract for themselves and their creation Mrs Beattie Bellman, née 'Lipman'. The monster was growing two heads.

It was the culmination of two years of mounting media attention for Beattie. Editors instructed their journalists to find out how many telephones I had, how many telephones my mother had, how often we use them, what model? A reporter scurried up to my mother's house in Hull on the pretext of an interview in *Bella*, only to sell it to the *Daily Mail* for a double-page spread on Beattie's real mother, where the real mother in question was quoted as saying she used Mercury because it was cheaper. The real mother then *opened* a telephone shop in her native town for a fee. A magazine showed me on a walkabout phone – clearly not a BT model – also showing my phone number. After some weeks of hilarious phone calls from their deeply witty readership my entire phone system was 'Telecom'd' and I found myself the proud owner of three switch boards, two lines, 13 phones and a 12 ton phone box. All for a five bedroom house! (On behalf of my 15-year-old daughter and the rest of us who occasionally make a call, I'd like to thank Crouch End Customer Service!)

It had taken me twenty-two years to reach Beattie-fication. Quite a long time spent in theatre and TV, rep and national companies, always trying to work new ground and play different characters. Above all never to be stereotyped. Twenty-two years to be known primarily as a white haired Jewish GRANDMA with a sharp tongue, a warm heart, and a fatal obsession with food and family. A household name – like Harpic. Twenty-two years to be greeted by one and all with, 'You look so much younger in real life' and to find myself on the financial pages of *The Times* alongside a report of BT's quarterly profits.

Don't get me wrong. I'm not knocking its success. The commercials are funny, well made, and they prove a point. That with all the techn'ology involved in advertisements – all the angles and video cutting – what the public actually want to see, and always remembers, is characterization, plot and relationships – like in a play.

But back to the beginning. It all started with a phone call to my agents. Apparently I was on the wanted list for the part of the as-yet-unnamed Grandmother, so I agreed to meet the people from the advertising agency. Now, I don't know who they'd seen before me, but I gather it was quite a few. I was obviously too young by twenty years, too thin by half and, as they would find out, too opinionated by plenty. On the plus side I knew the character as well as I knew my son's sock drawer – why shouldn't I? I'd lived with her for 18 years and been chained to the phone by her for the other 22, and I seemed to get on well from an ideas point of view with the prima donnas who would be behind the campaign. At the end of the meeting I felt that *they* felt they had their 'momma'. My agent was in seventh heaven – and on 15% why shouldn't he be. My son began negotiations for a dinghy with outboard motor for the swimming pool he felt we should be adding.

Then, two weeks later, they announce they want to do a 'test'. I say no. Vi Shilling, wardrobe, an old friend, says it's only for wig and make-up, so I say yes.

It was a riot. I was dressed in an over-the-top silk blouse, winged spectacles, heavy make-up and a gunmetal bouffant wig. I looked rather like everyone's favourite Auntie Freda, the one who ran a gown shop in Temple Fortune and never asked anyone for a favour. As far as the Beattie we now know and tremble in front of, she was very much mark one.

It was clear from the beginning that this was no mere wig and make-up test. It was an audition without a script. I took several deep breaths, contemplated telling them to shove it, then – remembering the school fees – launched into a sort of 'clap hands here comes forty years of showing off in public', at your service with a smile, a song, a joke, some with an ethnic slant – we fill the stage with bagels! By the time I'd finished, I suppose the camera had been whirring for over an hour, and the over-the-top silk blouse was wet through and sticking to the actress in question like a T-shirt to Linda Lusardi.

But they must have liked it. Because the following day 'the deal' was agreed and a short time later I started work at Wembley studios.

Meanwhile, they were still looking for someone to play Harry, the husband – you know the old joke – *son:* 'Momma, I got the part! I'm playing the husband!' *mother:* 'You couldn't get a speaking part?' I'd worked with Geoffrey Chiswick in a BBC play called *Shiftwork* and I suggested he might be just the fellow for the mission. This left the youngest grandson, Oliver, 'a voice like an angel' to cast.

A couple of days before filming began it was Yom Kippur, the Day of Atonement. It's a long and hungry day and it's best spent in the synagogue, participating in the service, in order to forget and forego your longings for braised steak and onions.

During a break I saw a small boy shinning up a pillar. I asked him his name. 'Alistair,' he replied in mid-shin. 'And do you like acting, Alistair?' He picked his lip thoughtfully, 'well I was a sheep once in the Christmas play, but I never got any lines!' I wrote a note to his mother and the next day they hired him.

And so to the 'shoot'. The director was Tony Smith, who'd made *Tutti Frutti*. He was an actor's director. Concise and economic, he kept my performance small. The 'Mrs Jones' script went like a dream. The crew, a single personality on a set, quietly came round to his point of view.

We were working flat out. One evening we filmed a commercial at six o'clock, the script for which I'd been handed at five o'clock. It was a monologue called 'Good News'. In it Beattie poured gratitude for some fabulous piece of good news into the ear of a young man called Clive, 'Oh that *is* good news – that's the best thing I've heard all day! What do I mean? It's the best thing I've heard all year! Oh Clive I *am* grateful' etc. etc. The punchline was to Harry: 'It's alright – he's had a cancellation for a tint. He's fitting me in.' Simple enough. But Tony had me pacing back and forth in front of a small mantel mirror and filmed me through the mirror. It was incredibly complicated to say exactly the same word at either side of the mirror each time to enable me to walk back to the mirror for the key words which had to be seen. It was, without question, the hardest and most technical piece of acting I've ever done. King Lear would have been a piece de gâteau! It was never shown.

On Thursday, in spite of Michael Fish, we had the great hurricane. I of course, experiencing hurricanes of one kind or another all week, slept right through it. The next morning, George, my driver, called at seven o'clock and we drove in shock across the whole of London from Muswell Hill to Battersea. It looked like World War 3. A huge poplar down in a garden; great shattered monsters lying uprooted and all over Hampstead Heath making the roads impassable; Regent's Park – a cemetery; Hyde Park . . . Battersea Park! We were numb.

As I dressed as Beattie for a Phonecard ad with Zia Mohyeddin, the sun was shining brilliantly. We shot a few seconds then the weather changed dramatically and driving rain and gloom fell. A canopy went over the camera bit in the end and we abandoned work and that particular ad never really recovered.

I got home to see my housekeeper Yvonne's boyfriend had arrived from Wales. Normally, this didn't fill me with delight, but this time he was up on my roof putting back the slates. It's an ill hurricane . . .

One more day and it was over. In a little over two weeks we had shot ten commercials. Then I went home, dropped more flowers at the Old People's home and collapsed in a heap. The diary reads: 'I've done it. Badly – but I've done it'. Gradually, the ads were shown and the consensus seemed to prove the diary wrong.

After JWT won the International contract, the next move was to widen Beattie's family. Enter a Canadian brother Lionel and a sister Rose in Australia. It seemed fairly clear that Lionel needed to be played by an actor from across the water, but Rose? Wouldn't it be fun to dress up the same but different and affect an Antipodean accent? The agency loved the idea. But guess what? Would I be willing to do a test?

So Viv and I went 'Kanga' and Rose emerged with a red wig, blue contact lenses, and a smart line in three piece knits and heavy gilt costume jewellery. True to form, Richard Phillips took one look at the test and decided it was all wrong. Only the blue contact lenses survived.

Anyway, one thing led to another and in no time at all, I had the Qantas tickets in my hand and two weeks in the sun were gleefully anticipated.

The diary reads: 'The first day's filming took place in a garden overlooking Sydney Harbour. The bridge was growing out of my shoulders and the Opera House looked like a hair ornament. I was wearing a fetching array of grey wig, blue contact lenses, pink sun visor, a yard of padding in my sun dress and two wads of sponge in my cheeks to fatten them out. I was sipping a cool guava juice. The only slight drawback was the howling wind and the blinding rain coursing relentlessly down on the heavy plastic sheeting over the camera and the sizzling of the cue lamps burning down to simulate Australian weather. I gripped the sides of my garden chair to prevent myself being blown onto Bondi Beach, and at 4 o'clock we abandoned all hope and headed back to the hotel, the proud possessor, as were the rest of the crew, of the long brown Australian mac known as a 'Driza-bone'. Wistfully I phoned England to be told the weather was in the 70s and they were out having a 'barbie'. Actually we had a ball. Being together on location has turned a motley crew into a company and the next commercials we do should be a treat.'

Well the next commercials we did *were* a treat. Albeit a late night treat. We worked from 7–10 at night and till 2 in the morning on the night shoot. We've reached, I think, a watershed in Beattie-tudes. I'm over my paranoia that she's taking over my life – Dorian Grey-wig-wise. I've accepted the fact that if I'm opening in Lourdes in a play about Sister O'Grady of the Convent of Sacred Hearts the press will ask me how being Jewish affects my daily life.

The fact is, she's funny. Beattie is funny. The story so far is funny, the awards are funny, (you should see them! as I said at the Golden Break awards: 'Awards are like Haemorrhoids – sooner or later every bum gets one.') and with a bit of luck – and an extended deadline – this book will be funny too. If not, do me a favour, don't phone to tell me.

Beattie
Mark One

Extracts from the fateful day when I first tried out for the part. . . not so much improvisation as desperation.

'Are we on the air? 'Cause he said to me: "Come along for a test." and I didn't exactly know what a test was, so I'm here and er . . .' I put down my only prop, a cup of tea, and looked at the ocean of faces looking straight back at me.

'I don't have lipstick on my teeth do I?' There followed two well documented Jewish jokes, both of which had cropped up in my book *How Was it For You?* a couple of years before, one concerning a vase and the other a gorilla. The camera operator began to shake and the studio erupted into laughter. I began to enjoy myself. 'So all of a sudden – it's turned into a show!' Then: 'Hello operator? Helloo – is anybody on the job? Operator, I want Greenmans the Kosher Butcher, I want some meat for the weekend. My son's coming and I can't get through. Thank you dear – Hello? Hello? Hello Clive, how are you? Oh very thank you dear. I want a nice piece of brisket for a casserole. No fat. How's the baby? Aah! Aah is she? Aah already? Bless her? Mine? Very well, thank you, all of them prodigies. I want some liver and I want it thinly sliced. Calves'! What do you mean what sort? You didn't think I mean pigs' did you eh? (laughs) How's your mother since the . . .? Ooh I *am* sorry. Oh dear – *all* out – oh I am sorry, well a lot of people manage with just the one . . . and have you got the frying sausages? I'll have 24 in two separate bags for the freezer. The big ones. Listen I've got to go there's someone at the door, you'll send that round will you? If I'm not in you can leave it with her next door – she's not bad . . . . Bye Bye Clive, thank you very much, Bye Bye.'

(Help! There was a silence, I racked my brains for inspiration.) 'So what about the new rabbi eh? Did you hear what happened? Well you know of course that Percy Wacholder died just as the new rabbi arrived in the town.

Well of course it was difficult for him not knowing Percy personally – listen, it was difficult if you *did* know Percy . . . So he stands up at the house of mourning and he asks for someone to say a few words about the late Percy Wacholder and of course – well you know what it is – nobody said a word. Well what could ya say? He was the biggest . . . Well, yes, but the man died and something had to be said, so he asks again "Will someone, anyone, say a few words – a syllable – about the late Percy Wacholder?" And again, not a murmur – terrible thing. Finally he said "I appeal to you for the last time. You knew the man – I didn't. I would *like* to say something about him, but I can't. Will someone *please* say something – anything – about the late Percy Wacholder." Finally, at the back of the room, an old man raised himself from his seat, looked around the room, sighed, and said "His brother was worse."

And then it was over. And then they changed my wig, changed my wardrobe, changed just about everything. Other than that they liked it.

Rose By Any Other Name
Mark One

Selected bits and pieces from my first attempt at playing the sister who buzzed off to Australia. (If you had a sister like Beattie, wouldn't *you*?) Performed in a muted Strine. 'We want a character who left England about 30 years ago, not a native Australian.' they said 'Thirty I'm not so good at' I replied 'I'll try twenty nine!'

'Beattie? Oh she's a lovely woman – she's got a beaut here, really beaut. And she means well you know. She's a little older than I am and you know I think it shows. I'm not saying that in an unkind way, I just think she doesn't have to let herself go so much. She could take more exercise. Maybe a little cosmetic help. You know it can give you a lift. And tips and streaks wouldn't kill her. There's always been Beattie for me though – she still holds my hand when we cross the road, it's ridiculous really.

I think I've got a bit of a sniffle you know. I don't know if you can notice? Does it matter for the programme? Is the make-up girl here – Lorna is my nose red? It'll pick up because there's red in my gown.

I don't know if Beattie would like it over here. Everybody wants to come now 'cos it's clean and beautiful and we've got no nuclear whatsit. We recycle a lot of things here, did you know that? We do. We only use biodegradable here and only white toilet rolls. Well of course, because the green and blue ones kill the fish. We care over here, we really do – I love it here. I've never missed the old country not one bit. I don't think I've got a London accent at all, do you? Although people here call me a real Pom, after all these years. My husband Cyril used to work in swimming pool filters and there's a marvellous future in it, but he got tired of it and went into carpets. I used to have a gown shop but now I play bridge and Kaluki and tennis. I go to the salon every week for a pedicure and I take care of my nails. I don't have time for work I really don't.'

Looked beaut, didn't I? The agency didn't think so. They wanted more wrinkles. So out went the red wig, and on went the grey and down-under, down market went her clothes – and down market went I.

FAMILY TREE

(Far From Which the Apple Doesn't Fall)

Harry
(Geoffrey Chiswick)

Beattie
(Maureen Lipman)

Melvyn
(Linal Haft)

Bernice
(Christina Avery)

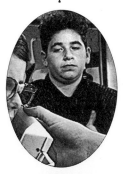

Anthony
(Jacob Krichefski)

Oliver
(Alistair Kent)

Natalie
(Hayley Napper)

Rose
(Maureen Lipman)

Cyril
(Clive Swift)

Lionel
(Brian Greene)

Norma
(Sandra Caron)

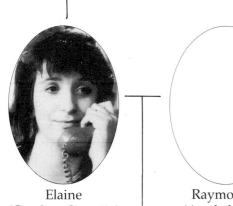

Elaine
(Caroline Quentin)

Raymond
(Apply here)

Zara
(Kate Orton)

BEATTIE'S HOUSEHOLD HINTS

A few drops of lemon added to cream when whipping, helps to stiffen the cream quicker. Now, of course, you can buy it in a tin ready whipped, but to me it tastes like shaving cream – which is not something I'm in the habit of putting on my strudel.

A few drops of lemon juice added to rice when boiling makes it very white, and also prevents grains from sticking together. If I'd know that before I encountered Uncle Ben!

Never throw away water in which potatoes, carrots or onions have been boiled – it makes a splendid basis for gravies and soups. There was always a stock pot on my mother's stove. This was in the days when Mr Heinz was still a glint in his father's eyes.

When buying tinned foods, mark the tins with the date you bought them, and use them in date order. Check through with a sieve for foreign bodies put there by animal rights meshugennas.

Always place large casseroles on a baking tray when cooking in the oven. They are then easier to remove from the oven, with less risk of breakage. Also, remove your glasses before removing casserole for fear of steaming up and walking into your next of kin.

When weighing golden syrup, sprinkle the scale with flour before putting in the syrup; it will then slip nicely off the scale. This will change your life!

When boiling cauliflower, add 1 teaspoonful of sugar to the water, it will then stay a good colour – not that it's such a wonderful colour to begin with!

Anthony and the Ology

Melvyn
(the Telephobic Son)

A Voice Like an Angell

Not Keeping Up With
the Joneses

Anthony and the Ology

Beattie's grandson, the scholar, is awaiting his results. His grandmother, who considers it her sacred duty to give unyielding support, whether it's wanted or not, baked him a somewhat premature congratulatory cake. Unable to bear the silence of her kitchen – now the oven has stopped groaning – she gives him a ring.

Beattie: 'Hello Anthony, congratulations on your exam results.'

The scene at the other end is not the ticker-tape celebration she fondly imagines. For Anthony, being a chip off the old block, has inherited much of the paternal sawdust . . .

Anthony: 'Grandma, I failed.'

'Failed' is a word which has no place in Beattie's frame of reference.

Beattie: 'You failed? What do you mean you failed?'

(Beattie) There must be some kind of explanation. He can't mean what he says.

Anthony: 'I mean I failed. Maths, English, Physics, Geography, German, Woodwork, Art. I failed.'

(Beattie absently removes the marzipan scroll so lovingly, optimistically resting on the cake.)

(Beattie thinks) Listen, no sense in wasting perfectly good cake. It can be adapted for other occasions . . .

Beattie: 'You didn't pass anything?'

Anthony: 'Pottery.'

(Beattie) My grandson – the artist. Is this maybe, what Picasso's grandmother had to listen to on the phone one day? or Mrs Tretchicoff? The boy needs reassurance. There's no stigma in being a sensitive genius whose work will one day be displayed in Selfridges basement!

Beattie: 'Pottery, very useful, Anthony, people will always need plates!'

(Beattie) It's so simple when you use the power of logic. Now let us continue to look on the bright side – and while I'm looking I'll pop back the scroll – who knows? Maybe I could make a paint brush and palette out of glacé cherries . . .

Beattie: 'Anything else?'

Anthony: 'And Sociology'

(Beattie) Under a bushel he hides his light!

Beattie: 'An Ology. He gets an ology and he says he's failed.'

(Beattie) Looks, brains, charm, artistic genius AND modesty to a fault! Bless him, it's no coincidence that his first name has the same initial as Einstein's . . .

'. . . You get an ology you're a scientist.'

(Beattie) Two brilliant results. Obviously the other marks were wrong – a travesty! No wonder the teachers go on strike – they're all illiterate! They can't recognize a genius when it's staring them in the mortar board!

Beattie: 'It's the teachers that are wrong. You know they can't mark. A lot of them can't see . . .'

(Beattie) You'll show them Anthony – you'll have plate exhibitions all over the world – you'll be the plate king of Europe – you'll marry a nice Jewish socialite. She'll be dressed by the Emmanuels, she'll have her nose fixed by the finest surgeon in California – you'll live in a house fit for an Ologist – with a lake and a moat – and will you have a dinner service!!!

Melvyn (the Telephobic Son)

(Beattie thinks) Ah – a bit of peace and quiet at last. Harry's at the club. I can just relax and think about nothing for a change. No worries – nothing on my mind . . . The kids are all well. Thank God . . .

Beattie: 'So you can't phone . . .'

(Beattie) I've got a wonderful family. I'm a very lucky woman. Always something going on, friends, family, kids . . . grandchildren . . .

Beattie: '. . . You can't pick up the phone and dial . . .'

(Beattie) They all phone, call round, all of them. Every one. Well, most of them . . .

Beattie: '. . . You've got maybe something wrong with your finger . . .'

Melvyn (the Telephobic Son)

(Beattie) And Melvyn . . . I can take or leave. In his own time he does things . . .

Beattie: '. . . It's an allergic reaction to the telephone?'

(Beattie) He's a busy boy – always was, a lot on his mind – a wife – kids, he married too young but . . .

Beattie: '. . . A phobia . . . you're telephobic.'

(Sound effects: Dialling.)

Melvyn: 'Hello, Mum.'

(Beattie) From my mouth to God's ears . . .

(Sound effects: Phone being put down.)

After.

Melvyn (the Telephobic Son)

Beattie: 'So you can't visit. You can't come round, you can only phone.'

Beattie: 'Never mind.'

(Beattie) But I'll stay as cool as a sweet and sour cucumber.

Beattie: '. . . It's a pleasure to hear your voice.'

(Beattie) Wild horses wouldn't drag a complaint out of me.

Melvyn (the Telephobic Son)

Beattie: '... A little more often wouldn't hurt.'

A Voice Like an Angel!

(Sound effects: Phone ringing.)

(Beattie thinks) Whoever it is I'll make no mention of the fact that it's my birthday.

Beattie: 'Hello.'

Oliver: 'Happy Birthday ...'

(Beattie) Bless him – how did they remember?

Oliver: '... to you ...'

(Oliver) I'm doing this for one reason only ...

Oliver '... Happy Birthday ...'

A Voice Like an Angel!

(Bernice) *It's not my side of the family he gets his stubbornness from.*

Oliver '. . . to you . . .'

(Beattie) *Bless him – his own idea, it must have been – bless him.*

Oliver: '. . . Happy . . .'

(Harry) *What's the matter with her? It looks like bad news . . .*

Oliver: '. . . Birthday . . .'

(Oliver) *Why me? This is indescribably tacky and boring – not even for a rotten Mars Bar am I going to continue . . .*

(Bernice) *Your father will kill you.*

A Voice Like an Angel!

(Melvyn) I'll kill him.

(Anthony) I had to bloody do it for 5 years and so will you – or I'll pulverize you – you spoilt toerag!

Oliver: 'Dear Grandma . . .'

(Oliver) If I don't finish I'm a dead boy.

Oliver: '. . . Happy Birthday to you.'

(Beattie) It's music to a grandmother's ears – and the feeling behind it . . .

Beattie: 'A voice like an angel!'

(Beattie) Bless him. Bless them all. Even her. It's what life's all about. I'm a very lucky woman – my cup brimmeth over.

A Voice Like an Angel!

(Beattie) I can feel myself going – I mustn't let them know I'm moved – they'll be upset.

Beattie: 'I'm very happy. You tell them.'

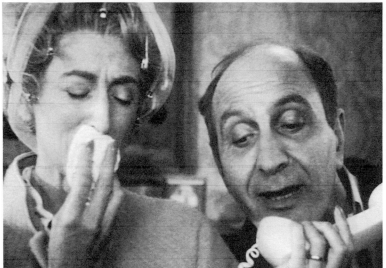

Harry: 'Your grandmother's very happy.'

(Harry) You can tell that because she's blubbing all over her dressing gown . . . Thank God she's happy, she'll forget how old she is . . .

Beattie: 'I'm very happy.'

(Harry) She's forgotten.

The last day of the sale and Beattie has been 'meaning to go'. After several hours spent 'weighing up' the various merits, she settles on the washing machine she knew she would get when she came in the store.

Beattie: 'Oh, are you there? I'm interested in this washing machine.'

'Interested', you'll note – one step further than 'I'm just looking.'

Sales Asst 1: 'I'm sorry, madam, this one's been reserved.'

(Beattie thinks) What is this, a restaurant?

Beattie: 'Reserved!'

Sales Asst 1: 'Yes, by a Mrs Jones. She telephoned earlier this morning.'

(Beattie) Listen, maybe it's a good thing it's gone already. My top loader's got years left in it still. What I really *need* replacing is my Hoover – mine doesn't pick up like it used to – listen, after 20 years who does?

Beattie: 'Oh, young man. Could I take this one, please?'

Sales Asst 2: 'Certainly.'

Sales Asst 3: 'Sorry, George. That's reserved. Mrs Jones has just phoned.'

(Beattie) This Mrs Jones appears to have some kind of a monopoly. Also an empty house by the sound of it . . .

(Beattie) Maybe what I should be looking at is an oven – I'm still using my mother's New World – Old World it should read. Now this one . . .

Beattie: 'Very nice. I've decided I'll take it.'

Sales Asst 4: 'Sorry, madam, a Mrs Jones reserved this by phone.'

Beattie: 'He's here again with his Mrs Jones!'

(Beattie) This woman has a hot-line to the world of electricity!

(Beattie) I'll bet she's reserved a dishwasher as well. I expect her husband wouldn't want her to soil her white hands with a pan scrub twice a day, three times since he's retired!

Beattie: 'And this one, is this also reserved for Mrs Jones?'

Sales Asst 4: 'No, madam, would you like it?'

(Beattie) Hallelujah! That's all I needed to know.

Beattie: 'No, thank you. If it's not good enough for Mrs Jones it's not good enough for me!'

BEATTIE'S HOUSEHOLD HINTS

To remove FAT stains, make a paste of Fullers Earth and water, and spread on stain. Allow to dry, and rub off. If you're on a fat-free diet ignore this tip.

Fruit and vegetable stains on hands can be removed by rubbing oatmeal moistened with lemon juice. Never use soap. The oat is a wonderful thing and the secret, also, of a wonderful skin.

To remove paint from windows, rub panes with hot vinegar. Ask your husband, if he's retired, to do the outsides. You can re-do them later.

To remove grass stains use a grease solvent, but dab it on sparingly. Alternatively, sponge with methylated spirit.

To remove scorch marks the best treatment is to wash with soapy water to which borax has been added, then gently rub in a little glycerine and wash again. (Who gets scorched these days since the advent of the gas-coal-log-effect fire?)

All furniture must be covered in dralon. You can clean *anything* off dralon.

Always wear a nylon bag over your head when frying fish.

Never accept Yes or No as an answer, this could well be the end of a conversation, say 'Do you really?'

When grandchildren come round switch off ballet on the TV as you can see men's abdomens.

A downstairs toilet is very important as you get older.

BEATTIE-FICATION

6.30 in the morning and all's hell.

Mother-to-be takes on grandmother-to-be (make-up by Lorna Magowan).

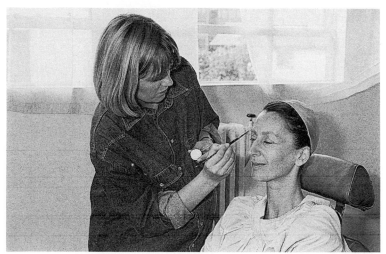

Isn't she lovely?

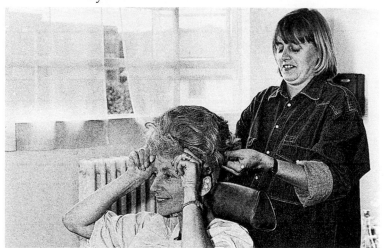

Now, that's much better.

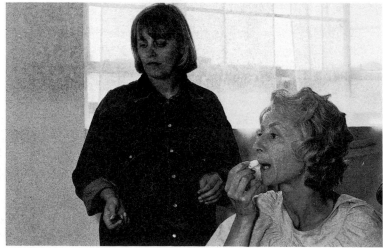

Feeling my age.

MDL – Maureen Diane
Lipman? No, Mutton
Dressed up as Lamb!

The bust is yet to come.

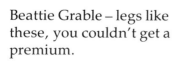

Beattie Grable – legs like these, you couldn't get a premium.

Just part of my á la mode collection. Diana should be so lucky!

Vi Shilling makes last minute adjustments – but what I say is, you can't improve on perfection.

Something for Nothing

A Parent's Woes

Sale (Or Return!)

The Answerphone

Presenter: 'Remember when dialling the numbers that those beginning with 0800 mean the call is free. The charge is paid by the people receiving the call.'

(Beattie thinks) That's very unusual. A little generosity goes a long way in a cold world.

Beattie: 'This I didn't know.'

Beattie: 'I thought those numbers . . .'

Beattie: '... always meant abroad.'

(Beattie) What a charming idea.

(Beattie) All those years I've been missing out – I've never checked to see if anyone I know has 0800 in front of their number.

Beattie: '... I wonder ...'

Presenter: 'However, this doesn't mean you can dial 0800 before just any number.'

Presenter: 'Only numbers which say they begin with 0800 are free.'

(Beattie) With the one hand they give – and with the other . . .

Beattie: 'You can't have everything.'

(Beattie) Mind you, it would be interesting to see . . . Well, why not? It can't hurt.

Beattie: 'NO, no, normally I wouldn't be interested in a thermo-insulated turbo pump . . .'

(Beattie, looking at Harry) What's he looking at? Ever since he retired all he does is look. He could take a degree in it. I'm doing business here and he's looking.

(Harry) Oh yes. A thermo-insulated turbo pump. Just what we need. Get one. Get two! We'll give up Fuengirola this year – get a houseful – maybe they'll breed!

Beattie: '. . . but in view of your kind offer I couldn't not call.'

(Beattie) Listen. It whiles away an afternoon . . .

A Parent's Woes

(Beattie thinks) What I'm doing in Streatham I don't know. Only a mother could love a daughter enough to travel across the whole of London to clean up what can only be described as a squat. I've got two kinds of bleach for her S-bend. Now, have I forgotten anything?

(Beattie) What's he sticking up? Is it an offer? Maybe you can win a cruise abroad with that bleach I've just bought.

Beattie: 'Oh, phonecards. Too complicated for what I need.'

(Newsagent) All my elderly ladies say the same thing – I must explain with the actions.

Newsagent: 'No, no, no. Phonecard most simple.'

(Beattie) He doesn't realize you can't teach an old dog new tricks.

Beattie: 'Really?'

Newsagent: 'Yes, look, look. I'll show you. Please, this way.'

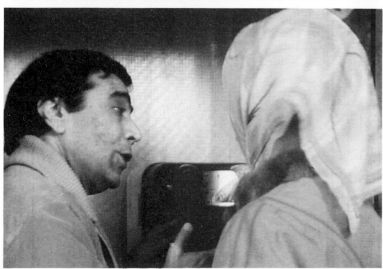

Newsagent: 'Phonecard in here.'

A Parent's Woes

Newsagent: 'Presto, hey!'

Newsagent: 'Phone call is over, card pops out.'

Beattie: 'Yes.'

(Beattie) Why is he talking to me as if I'm barmy?

Newsagent: 'Simple enough for you?'

Beattie: 'Well, simple enough for me. It's not me I'm thinking of. It's my son, Melvyn. He seems to have great difficulty in using the phone.'

(Beattie) I thought for his birthday I could buy him some phonecards, like a little hint. About a gross of them.

Newsagent: 'Oh, don't tell me. Children, you do everything for them, you work your fingers to the bone.'

(Beattie) It could be me talking . . .

Newsagent: 'And what do you get?'

Beattie: 'Nothing.'

Newsagent: 'They never phone.'

Beattie: 'No.'

Newsagent: 'They never write.'

Beattie: 'Never.'

Newsagent: 'They never fax.'

(Beattie) All over the five corners of the globe – children give you the same heartache

Sale (Or Return!)

Beattie: 'That's it, yes, yes, I want the size 14 in baby blue with the repeating sleeping pelican motif. And do you deliver?'

Sales Assistant: 'This morning?'

Beattie: 'This morning. Oh, good.'

(Beattie thinks) Oh – I should inquire – just in case.

Beattie: 'And are you open this afternoon?'

Sales Assistant: Well, madam, I thought you wanted it delivered this morning.

(Beattie) Aaah – They don't understand these days – so inexperienced. I'll be gentle with him.

Beattie: 'Young man, shopping by phone is all very well . . .'

(Beattie) That way he'll learn.

Beattie: '. . . but taking it back – that requires the personal touch.'

The Answerphone

(Melvyn thinks) I shouldn't have done it but I couldn't face going back to the office after that squash game. Off work early on a Friday – I'll be shot! No one's at home. Bernice is on the school run then the orthodontist. I hope there's something to eat in the house. Oh no! It's her day at the friendship club – there'll be sod all. Never mind, I'll have a scotch and soda and put my feet up. Must go to the bathroom. Any messages?

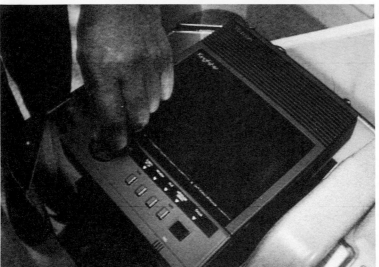

(Sound effects: Appropriate clicks and buzzes. Our heroine's voice is on the machine.)

(Melvyn) I'm looking fit, mind you – the exercise is doing me good.

(Sound effects: Beep, beep.)

(Melvyn) It'll be for Bernice or the kids. If there's one for me it'll be a miracle. Unless . . .

Beattie (reasonable): 'Melvyn. It's your mother. Call me back.'

(Melvyn) Later. Later. Much later, when I've got the strength.

(Sound effects: Beep, beep.)

Beattie (slightly firmer): 'Don't forget to call.'

(Melvyn) I'll call, I'll call. I'm starving. I need to be full before I call her – or she'll know.

(Sound effects: Beep, beep.)

Beattie (tone rising): 'Guess who? I still haven't heard from you, Melvyn.'

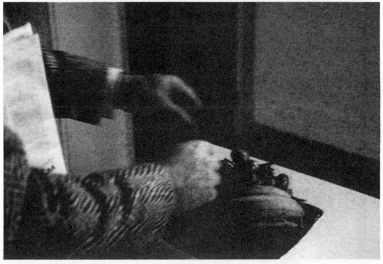

(Sound effects: Beep, beep.)

(Melvyn) It couldn't be. Not again.

Beattie (heavily sarcastic): 'Remember me, Melvyn?'

(Melvyn) It could be.

The Answerphone

Beattie: 'We spoke once – a very long time ago.'

(Melvyn) And for a very long time.

Beattie: 'I'm the one they call your mother.'

(Melvyn) Your sarcasm is not lost on me, mother. However, I am in my own home and an Englishman's home is his fortress.

(Melvyn) I'll call you in my own time . . .

(Sound effects: Phone ringing.)

(Melvyn) . . . because I'm a big boy now, mother.

(Melvyn) And big boys have to go to the bathroom when they need to.

Beattie (on answering machine, furious): 'Melvyn, I know you're in there.'

The Answerphone

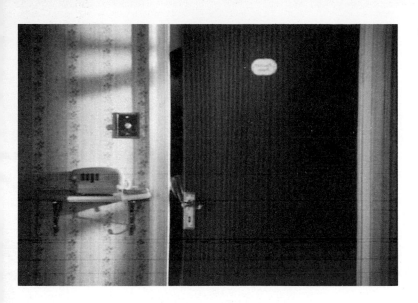

(Melvyn) She knows I'm in here.

Little Zara, my youngest grandchild, with my daughter Elaine. She's a sweet little thing but I can't help worrying. Elaine and Raymond have got such funny ideas. Look at that haircut! The poor child won't know whether she's Martha or Arthur.

Mr Edwin from Edwin Modes in the High Street. Not exactly Hardy Amies. In fact, judging by way he keeps bringing out the same old styles year after year, more like hardy annuals.

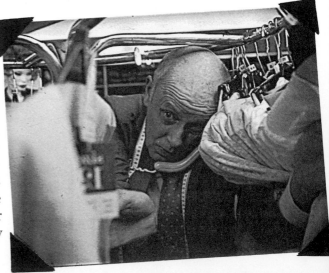

My brother Lionel in Toronto. With him being so far away, I worry about him a lot, but it's obvious that at least they have good dentists over there. (I had a picture of him with his wife Norma but to be honest, I never liked her.)

My sister Rose and brother-in-law Cyril in Sydney. She's got two children of her own, Wayne and Shane. So the boy's not doing as well as Melvyn and the girl's not married, she could still send me a picture.

BEATTIE'S HOUSEHOLD HINTS

Clean behind the radiators. Nobody else will.

Whatever present you give them, make sure you are able to take it back so you don't feel beholden.

Grandchildren are your life when you get older. Your children you love but your grandchildren you love greater than Cleopatra loved Spartacus.

A gardener is unnecessary when your husband is retired. However clipping the hedge is dangerous for him.

The centre of your house is your cooker and your medicine chest.

If you don't have a Marks and Spencer near you try to organize a rota with your friends. People can always drop a list in.

Always press new Barmitzvah suit. Why press it? From Burtons' window it's new?

A few useful phrases:
Aren't eggs useful?
Doesn't it soon get to ten to ten?
Are you there?
This is it.
That could have been me talking!

Always have a plastic runner in the hallway. This saves wear and tear on the carpet. (If there is a dent in the carpet you can take it back to the manufacturers you bought it from ten years ago and complain that it has worn funny. The Japanese have got it right taking their shoes off.)

The Call That Never
Came

Melvyn
(the Workaholic Son)

Do You Have a 12
in the Green?

We'll Meet Again

The Call That Never Came

(Sound effects: Door slamming, keys jangling.)

(Beattie thinks) Oy! Rain, people, pushing, shoving. Me feet are killing me. I hope he's going to put the kettle on, while I listen back . . .

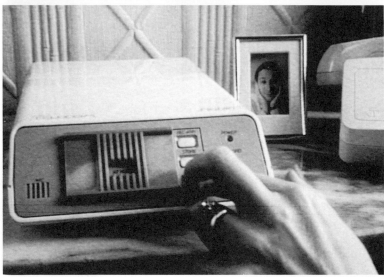

(Sound effects: Clicks and whirrs of answering machine.)

(Beattie) Marvellous. One touch and there's a whole world at your fingertips.

Message 1: 'It's Elaine here, Mum.'

(Beattie) Aaah – a daughter's a daughter the whole of your life – a son is a son till he takes him a wife. Never a truer word . . .

Elaine: 'Just rang to tell you Zara's tooth's through.'

(Beattie) Aaah, it's come through – and I wasn't there to see it. So advanced . . . takes after her grandmother.

Beattie: 'Ah . . . Bless her.'

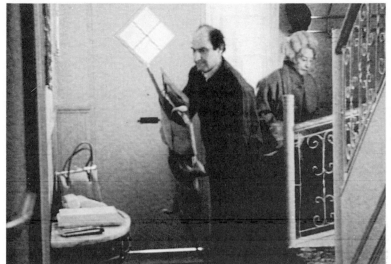

*(Beattie) What's he doing
with that ironing board?
He'll get a hernia. Oh, now
look, we're hooked up – he
can't just put the kettle on –
he's got to get under my feet.*

Message 2: 'This Ina Vista.
The easy-to-fit Austrian
blinds . . .'

*(Beattie) I was only inquiring
. . . there was no obligation.*

(Ina Vista) '. . . you inquired
about are now in stock.'

*(Harry) She's here with her
do-it-himself again . . .*

Harry: 'Easy for who!'

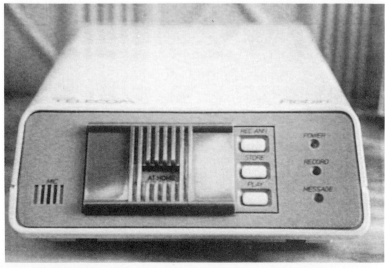

Message 3: 'It's Betty, dear,
don't go out tomorrow
afternoon. There's a Victor
Mature film on.'

*(Beattie) Aaah – she never
forgets . . . Knows the TV
Times off by heart like a
Bible. 'Course, she's nothing
else to do with herself – poor
soul . . .*

Beattie: 'Ooooooo.'

The Call That Never Came

(Beattie) That's it? That's all? It's cut out . . . I'll sue, it's brand new —

Beattie: 'Hello . . .'

(Beattie) Can it hear me?

Beattie: 'There's something wrong with this machine.'

Harry: 'Sounded all right to me.'

(Harry) As usual. Nothing's good enough. Who was she expecting, Michael Aspel?

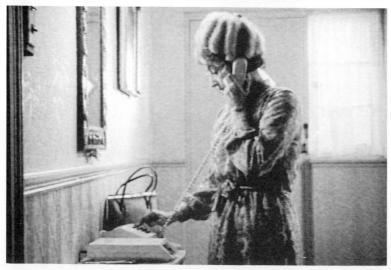

(Beattie) There's only one way to prove I'm right.

Beattie: 'Well, in that case.'

Melvyn: 'Hello.'

Beattie: 'Melvyn?'

> *(Beattie) Now. See? He'll prove it. One way or the other, I'll know . . .*

Beattie: 'I've just picked up my messages, I phoned as soon as I could!'

Melvyn: 'I didn't call you, Mum.'

> *(Beattie) As if I didn't know already – this machine is my witness . . .*

Beattie: 'Exactly Melvyn, exactly.'

> *(Beattie) . . . a little hint never hurt anybody.*

Melvyn (the Workaholic Son)

Melvyn: 'Hello, Mum? Look, I'm afraid we're going to be late.'

Beattie: 'You're going to be late?'

(Beattie thinks) Does he mean minutes? Hours? Should I put the meal on simmer? Is this a case for opening a new tube of Baco Foil?

Beattie (to Harry) '. . . he's going to be late!'

Harry: 'His sister's never late.'

(Beattie) He's right, but I'll let his father look like the villain!

Beattie: 'Your father says your sister's never late.'

Harry: 'She's got more consideration.'

(Harry) Watch her take his side against me.

*(Melvyn) It's not my fault!
Don't blame me – blame the
bosses. It's a* fait accompli.

Melvyn: 'I've got to work!'

Beattie: 'He's got to work.'

(Beattie) He says!

*(Beattie – thought strikes her)
My son is being exploited! By
the big bosses! And why?
Because he's the only one
who's too good to refuse to
work these hours.*

Beattie: 'I tell you this,
they're slavedrivers, those
people.'

(Melvyn) Before she starts . . .

Melvyn: 'I'll be an hour.'

Melvyn (the Workaholic Son)

(Beattie) An hour on an empty stomach. Working like a dog . . . for someone else? Never!

Beattie: 'I'll come down, I'll bring you a sandwich, your father will run me.'

(Beattie) At least I'll put him in the picture while I'm still on the phone, he'll not have a leg to stand on.

Beattie (to Harry): '. . . You'll run me.'

Melvyn: 'I don't want a sandwich! Are you there? No sandwich!'

(Beattie) He's raising his voice! He's hungry and lonely and cold – COLD!!! I should see this workhouse and have it condemned . . .

Beattie: 'I'll bring you a jumper. One of your father's.'

(Melvyn) Before she starts packing Duvets, thermal vests, and a balaclava . . .

Melvyn: 'I don't want a sandwich, I don't want a jumper, this is a modern air-conditioned building!'

(Beattie) Now I've got to see this office. Why has he never mentioned this before? This sounds worth a visit.

Beattie: 'Air-conditioned? You never told me it was air-conditioned.'

(Melvyn) Again I'm in trouble.

Melvyn: 'Why would I tell you?'

(Beattie) Weeks of worry he could have saved me – if he only told me important things.

Beattie: 'Melvyn, some children talk to their parents.'

(Beattie) Game, set and match – now I'll give him a wonderful reward!

Beattie: 'Now, what do you want in your sandwich?'

(Beattie) You see, if you'd only talk to me I would have known you were going to be held up in your fine office and I'd have brought the dinner in an insulated bag. This way I don't know . . .

Beattie: 'I've got that matured Canadian Cheddar that you like. I wish I'd known. I haven't got a lot in . . .'

Do You Have a 12 in the Green?

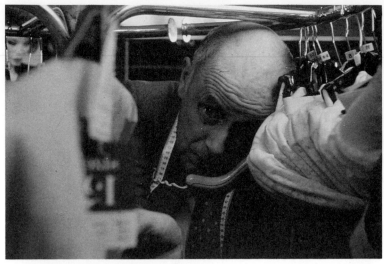

In a small but alarmingly chic ladies gown shop in Hendon High Street, a harassed sales person, on his own on a busy (but not busy enough) Saturday afternoon, is doing his utmost to assist a customer in her inquiries.

Shop Manager: 'Yes, yes, we have a 12 in the blue.'

But Beattie (for it is she) needs to double check that he understands the exact model to which she is referring – for fear of a wasted bus journey.

Beattie: 'With the scalloped neck?'

The manager wants nothing now but to complete this phone call and get back to his customers.

Shop Manager: 'Yes, a 12 in the blue with the scalloped neck.'

(Beattie thinks) I should also check the other colours. What if I get all the way there and I've gone off blue?

Beattie: 'And in the white?'

The manager cranes round the clothes rail and is thrilled to see at least two size 12s in the white.

Shop Manager: 'Yes, we have a 12 in the white.'

Beattie has mentally tried on both dresses and mentally found them dragging a bit across the chest.

Beattie: 'And do you have a 14 in the blue?'

The manager, who has mentally replaced his receiver, is somewhat put out to realize the inquiry has shifted into a new gear.

Shop Manager:'I thought madam was a 12?'

Beattie is delighted with the chance to explain the nature of the manufacturer's habit of pulling the wool over a customer's chest by making some size 12s fit a size 14, and vice versa, for their own amusement.

Beattie: 'Well, normally, yes, but you see if the cut is on the smallish side ... they're not generous these days ... you know what I mean, they skimp around the armholes.'

Do You Have a 12 in the Green?

The manager – fearing a further 5 or 10 minutes on the subject of skimping in relation to the human armpit – makes a return dive into the clothes rail.

Shop Manager: 'Yes, we have a 14 in the blue.'

Beattie – mentally trying on another two garments in the larger sizes.

Beattie: 'And in the white?'

The manager throws in the towel and gives madam the benefit of the size and colour of every dress on the rail. Now perhaps he can deal with his omnipresent customer.

Shop Manager: 'And in the white, and in the green, and in the pink.'

Beattie: 'Green? Oh . . .'

Beattie is intrigued by the new colour-range swirling into her mind's ear.

Beattie: 'Now, do you have a 12 in the green?'

The manager has bitten through most of his inner cheek.

Shop Manager: 'Yes, we have a 12 in the green.'

Beattie: 'And in the . . .?'

He bites through the rest of it and hears himself becoming hysterical.

Shop Manager: 'And in the pink!'

Do You Have a 12 in the Green?

Beattie, oblivious to either the manager's hysteria (must be a fault on the line) or his inner cheek, wants to re-cap.

Beattie: 'So, you've got all of the colours in all of the sizes?'

(Shop Manager thinks) Yess! Yess! The mindless twerp has got it!

Shop Manager: 'All of the colours in all of the sizes!'

Beattie cannot believe the availability of every size and colour she's inquired about. She's thrilled. And mystified.

Beattie: 'You haven't sold out of anything?'

(Shop Manager thinks) If this woman ever comes in to buy this dress, I will personally push each dress in each colour down her throat!

Shop Manager: 'Nothing at all!'

It slowly dawns on Beattie that the item in question is not a big seller.

Beattie: 'It's not what you'd call all the rage, is it?'

The manager assaults, scalps, and batters a perfectly innocent dummy . . . and feels no better for it.

(Beattie thinks) He'll faint when I tell him.

Beattie: 'I've just seen Leslie.'

(Harry) Hello – she's here with her intelligence tests again.

Harry:'Leslie? Leslie who?'

(Beattie) How many Leslies has he known? I hope he's not losing his short-term memory. That's all I'm short of.

Beattie: 'Your old friend Leslie. Saw him from the bus.'

Harry: 'Les ... Les! What, after all these years? No-oh.'

(Beattie) I can see him as if it was yesterday. He was the one I had my eye on when I met Harry.

Beattie: 'I did like Leslie. So charming.'

(Sound effects: Music)

(Beattie) Sitting on a stool in the Milky Way coffee bar with Eileen Silverstone and they walked in.

Straight away I thought – I like the one with the hat. I said to Eileen – 'I don't think much of yours' – just as she said it to me.

Beattie: 'Always used to ...'

Beattie: '. . . take his hat off.'

(Beattie) I nearly died when he started chatting up Eileen. As for Harry – he never said a word. Just ordered a frothy coffee and then played with the froth for half an hour.

Beattie: 'You never took your hat off.'

(Harry) I took my hat off to old Leslie though. What a mover!

Harry: 'Didn't have a hat.'

(Beattie) I can see him now, twisting his gold signet ring on his finger as he chatted up Eileen – all his nails were beautifully buffed, like Mother of Pearl.

Beattie: 'And he had wonderful hands too. Do you remember?'

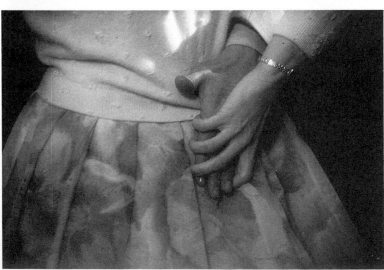

(Harry) Hands? I've seen those hands moving in fourteen different directions at the same time. Hands! Sleight of bloody hands he had!

Harry: 'He had wonderful hands all right.'

(Sound effects: Music)

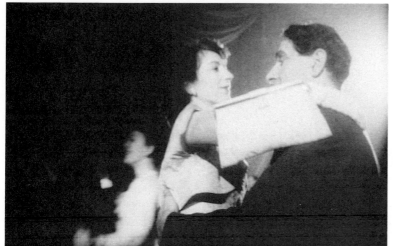

(Beattie) I used to watch him when we went to the Mecca in a foursome. He held a girl masterfully, firmly. Mind you, Harry was quite a good dancer in those days . . .

(Beattie) I wonder who he married? It wasn't Eileen, she married a Yank out of necessity. What was his last name now – I could look him up and give him a ring.

Harry: 'What're you doing?'

(Beattie) Imagine – a get-together after all these years.

Beattie: 'I was going to look and see if he was in the book.'

(Harry) If she's going to do it, it's better if I do it. He'll be thrilled to bits when he knows it's me.

Harry: 'Hello Les! It's Harry. Harry. *Harry*, Harry . . .'

(Harry) Clutz – he must be losing his short-term memory.

Harry: 'Yeh, yeh, yeh.'

Harry: '. . . She's just the same.'

(Beattie) He's mad! Just the same! I should be so lucky. Mind you . . . I've kept my figure and my teeth and that's what counts. I wonder what he'd think of me now? I wonder if he ever had a soft spot for me?

Harry (whispering): 'No, it's not Beryl. I never married Beryl.'

(Harry) If she finds out about Beryl Rabinowitz after all these years I'm a dead man. Sodding telephones! Who talked me into this?

A ROOM OF MY OWN

What you are seeing me in, in the photograph, is the through-room of my semi-detached bay windowed 1930s-built house in Wembley, North London. Harry and I have lived here for 32 years, ever since we left Stoke Newington, and our children Melvyn and Elaine lived here with us until Melvyn married beneath him, and Elaine dropped out. Melvyn's wife Bernice is a nice homely girl, at least he'll never have a problem with other men. We've solved both their cooking problems – they come to us.

I pride myself on the fact that as far as cleanliness is concerned my house is a palace. You could eat off the Dralon. I do have a woman in twice a week for a couple of hours but quite frankly by the time I've cleaned right through so it looks nice when she walks in, and listened to her tales of woe about the layabout she calls her 'common law' *and* cleaned up after her when she's left – I sometimes wonder why I bother at all, still, at least she's regular.

Since I had the two rooms knocked through this room has been a doddle, although since my husband retired I find it a little harder to keep it band-box as I like it, with him under my feet all day. I was concerned, initially, about the extra heating needed for such a big room, but once it was done, the dust had finally gone and I'd paid the unreliable cowboy builders, I must say I've been delighted with it. I also had them take out the fireplace, not the stone surround which I like, but the grate itself – Harry loved a real fire – but did he have to clean it? Or crouch down on the carpet with rolled up copies of the *Express* and a hair dryer to get it going? Anyway the electric fire was installed by a nice young man with naturally wavy hair from the Yellow Pages and I've never regretted it.

The wallpaper is a traditional pattern and I've had to search the five corners of the earth for duplicate rolls (thank heavens for the bus pass!) 'Discontinued' is not a word in my vocabulary. The carpet is entitled 'Subtle Sage' and I had it installed after the builders left. It's what they call a shallow shag-pile in Meraklan and Polyprolene which is a hundred per cent man-made fibre and, according to the salesperson, will last forever. I'm not entirely convinced – I've certainly been able to remove most of the vestiges of Harry's spilled nightcaps and my grandchildren's (bless them) Ribena – but I can't help noticing a certain bagginess in the lay since and I may have to get a man in. My staircarpet on the other hand is 80/20 and I couldn't fault it. The washed Persian rug in sage and coral was down before I went fitted – when I still had the parquet – and I wouldn't part with it. Apparently they are made absolutely perfect with just a single flaw. My husband on the other hand . . .

The three piece suite is also a trusty friend – it came from Maples in the early days of our marriage and we've shlepped it with us ever since. I've had it recovered in sage with a forest green piping which I've picked up in the embossed drapes – I'm a great believer in mix 'n' match – particularly without the mix, and I must say that Dralon's like a gift from the Lord rather than a fabric from Furnitureland. The antimacassars are a necessity. My husband favours Brylcream.

The Regency mahogany dining room suite was a present from Harry's mother Fay, God rest her soul. For years after she gave it, she continually threatened to take it back. In the end we bought her a replica and she complained on the grounds she'd wanted something 'High Teck'.

As you will see the circular gilt mantel mirror makes a set with the gilt, ormolu and inlaid enamel coffee table. They speak, I think, for themselves. A thing of Beattie is a joy for ever.

I don't have a great many ornaments, I think a surface should be free to breathe, but each one has a special meaning. The Crinoline figurines were brought back for me from Fuengirola by my dear friends Dolly and Gerald Green. A marriage made in Hendon. The odd chip in transit I never mentioned. Not everyone's budget runs to hard-shell luggage. The red Venetian glass bowl was a souvenir from a visit to a glass-blowing factory with the Friendship Club. Funnily enough, Essie Spearman wanted the same bowl and we haven't spoken since. Silly really – but I shan't be the first to phone.

Talking of which, I do have quite a modern telephone at each end of my through room. I had them changed to tone with the skirting boards when I last had the decorator in for a touch up. And of course the rubber plant is my pride and joy. Look how healthy and blooming it is. The leaves of your rubber do benefit from a drop of milk every so often you know. But then who doesn't?

Of course you are seeing my room of my own at its very best, because as of now it's technician free. Often I have to contend not only with Harry walking from room to room, jingling his pockets and asking when dinner's ready, but also up to maybe twenty assorted grips and sparks, clapper boys, focus pullers, riggers, continuity, producers, clients, the agency clients – oy a clog – I sometimes wonder where the next coconut macaroon is coming from.

Mind you, the chaos I can cope with, the arc lamps I can cope with – the constant cries of 'Action! Cut! Print! Mark it' I can cope with. Even when they remove my living room wall all of a sudden without so much as a by your leave, or paste white double-sided all over my parquet. All that I can stand. Just. But the one thing I *can't* stand, the one thing that makes me wish I'd stayed in Stoke Newington and never become a legend, pardon my language, and never had a Royal baby named after me, is that blooming woman Maureen Lipton with her wigs and her glasses and her padding and her ad-libs and her husband and her kids and her au pairs and her mother! I know she's a necessary evil but, quite frankly, if it wasn't for her constantly hogging the lamplight, this room of my own would be a haven of peace, contentment, and Lavender air freshener.

RITA PEARLMAN'S FLORENTINES

½ cup icing sugar
1 cup dried mixed fruit
glacé cherries
chocolate

1 cup mixed nuts (chopped)
white of an egg
a few drops of cream

Method: Line 2 flat baking tins with rice paper. Mix all ingredients thoroughly. Spoon 1 teaspoonful of mixture onto rice paper, leaving room between each spoonful, (I don't mean you have to go outside or anything – just widely space the Florentines!) Bake for 15 mins with melted chocolate.

JEAN ABRAHAM'S STUFFED MONKEYS
(don't ask me why – I've no idea – but they're a wonderful standby)

2 heaped cups flour
2 tablespoons sugar
¼ lb butter
1 large tablespoon cream
Filling:
½ lb dates
¼ lb sultanas
¼ lb currants
1 tablespoon butter

2 teaspoons baking powder
1 teaspoon vanilla
2 eggs

1 teaspoon vanilla
½ lb chopped nuts
2 tbls cinnamon and sugar

Method: Place flour, baking powder, sugar and vanilla in basin, and rub in butter. Cream with finger tips, add eggs and mix into a soft dough for rolling out. Chop all filling ingredients and mix together. Roll out dough into strips wide enough to turn after filling has been placed in them. Brush with milk and sugar and cinnamon mixture, and bake in moderate oven. When cooled off, cut into squares.

BEATTIE'S HOUSEHOLD HINTS

Windows are very important. When your husband retires, all he does is jingle his money in his pockets, so he can clean an inside window (it doesn't hurt). You can do it again later.

Have your hair set on big rollers once a week and wear a nylon mop cap at night.

Clean paint work as you go along. Always have a J-cloth to hand, it doesn't take much time, just rub as you go. By the time you get downstairs your husband will have made a nice cup of tea.

Every window must have a net curtain. A window without a net curtain is like a pope without a chalice.

Flowers are unnecessary in a house. They die. Get a plant – in a self-watering pot.

Remember as you get older your children have their own interests – take up kalooki.

Have lino in your bathroom as carpets encourage verrucas.

Always be at a railway station two hours early. If you do go away pack a week early. This you do on your own. Then you can pack and re-pack as often as is necessary. When he doesn't know where anything is, complain how often you packed.

Clean the house *before* your cleaner comes (and after) as they put everything in the wrong place and leave the lid off the cleanser to show they've been.

Crazy pave everything, even over the lawn, it looks neater. Then you don't argue with the man jingling his money about not mowing it.

Good News

The Dangling Fiancée

Have Phone Will Travel

Such Devoted Sisters

Beattie: 'Oh, Clive, that's
wonderful news. That's
marvellous. I'm thrilled to
bits. Well, yes, you must be.
Yes. Yes? No. Of course I am.
It's the best news I've had all
day. Well, I'm thrilled, I really
am. What a turn up, eh! You
know what they say – it's an
ill wind . . . You what? I said
it's an ill w. . . .eh? Yes. No.
I'm over the moon, I really
am. Oh, I can't tell you what
this means to me, Clive,
you've made my day. Listen,
you've made my year. Fate is
a wonderful thing. Well, this
is it. You can never tell. Bless
you, Clive, and thank you for
phoning. I'm as pleased as
punch. Bye bye, dear. Thank
you. Bye bye. Bye.'

*Beattie puts the phone
down and notices, as
she pats her perfect hair
in the lounge mirror,
that Harry is giving her
one of his looks. I
suppose he'll have to
know sooner or later.*

Beattie: 'It's Clive, he's had a
cancellation for a tint. He's
squeezing me in.'

The Dangling Fiancée

(Engineer thinks) Just another day. Just another call . . .

(Beattie) A total stranger comes into the house and Harry can't even put his jacket on – what will the young man think . . .?

Beattie: 'Excuse the tip, my husband's been home nearly twenty minutes.'

Engineer: 'Well, what's the trouble?'

(Engineer) Please let it be something I've got on the van.

(Beattie) I'll minimize the extreme seriousness of the problem.

Beattie: 'Stone dead, for hours. Do you know, I've almost forgotten how to speak.'

(Harry) I wonder how long
this job is going to be – does
he charge by the hour?

Harry: 'I've often said we
ought to buy the phone.'

(Beattie) He's got no tact!
Why antagonize a workman
when he's on the job?

Beattie: 'And would you get
the on-the-spot service
included? Go on, tell him.'

Engineer: 'Well, no.'

Beattie: 'So we're renting.'

(Beattie) He'll feel better if he
knows that. Better still after a
nice cup of tea and a stuffed
monkey. Poor boy looks thin
and tired . . .

Beattie (to engineer): 'When
you've done that, phone your
wife. Tell her that you're
going to be a bit . . .'

The Dangling Fiancée

Engineer: 'I'm not married.'

(Beattie) How can this be? No one looks after him? He's not, I hope – a bit – you know . . .

Beattie: 'You're not married! You've got a fiancée?'

(Engineer) Poor soul, she must be lonely – or just nosy.

Engineer: 'Well, a girlfriend. Three years now.'

(Engineer) That's fixed it. Ringing sounds normal – I'll make the complete programme if I scarper . . .

Engineer: 'It's working.'

(Beattie) I'll show him a little gratitude – makes all the difference.

Beattie: 'Good. Now you can phone your girlfriend.'

The Dangling Fiancée

(Engineer) Batty. She must be. Humour her.

Engineer: 'Sandra? I'm on my way . . .'

(Beattie) This girl must be told. This is a clever boy. Pleasant-looking, a trade at his fingertips – just needs the right encouragement – I'll have a word. She'll thank me one day.

Beattie: 'Sandra? You're keeping a lovely boy dangling. You wait for Victor Mature, you wait a long time, believe me.'

(Beattie) There. He's fixed my breakdown in communications, and I've fixed his. That's what we're in this world for, isn't it? To lend a helping hand to your fellow man.

(Original script by Paul Chown.)

After an afternoon at Melvyn and what's-her-name's, Beattie is being given a lift home. The goodbyes have taken just under an hour. Melvyn has had his coat on throughout. At the door Beattie remembers to forewarn her husband of her imminent arrival. She couldn't pass a phone and not do so.

Beattie: 'Harry, I'm on my way.'

Once in the car Beattie cannot believe the evidence before her eyes . . .

Beattie: 'A phone?'

Melvyn had a feeling she'd notice. He couldn't wait to get in the car and be nonchalant about it . . .

Melvyn: 'Business. I've just bought it. You've got to have one.'

(Beattie thinks) How well this boy of mine is doing goes without comment – but is this phone ONLY a business line or . . .

Beattie: 'Business, but can you use it for – er – normal life?'

Melvyn: 'Go on, give someone a call.'

(Beattie) The way to a mother's heart is through her ear . . .

(Beattie) When I was brought up, it wasn't considered 'nice' to accept an invitation too quickly . . .

Beattie: 'Oh, I don't like . . .'

(Beattie) But you've got to keep up with the times . . .

Beattie: 'Well . . . all right.'

(Sound effects: Phone rings.)

(Beattie) It's miraculous!

Harry: 'Hello?'

Beattie: 'Harry?'

(Beattie) It got through! This he won't believe!

Beattie: '. . . I'm on my way.'

(Harry) I'm having a déjà view!

Harry: 'I know you're on your way.'

Beattie: 'No, I'm on my way, I'm in the car.'

(Beattie) It's modern technology – it's beyond your father's apprehension!

Beattie: 'Melvyn's got a phone in the car.'

(Beattie) Look, look – give a look – she's looking with pure envy all over her face.

Beattie: 'I'll see you soon . . .'

(Beattie) Me – I don't need to show off – each to his own.

Beattie: 'Over and out.'

Beattie: 'You'll come in for a cup of tea?'

(Beattie) How often do I get him to myself?

Melvyn: 'Yeh, I'll come in for a cup of tea.'

(Beattie) I should have told Harry to put the kettle on. I'll do it now. It'll save a couple of seconds.

Beattie: 'Harry, put the kettle on.'

(Beattie) Who would have a bad word to say about the modern world of communications as we know it?

(original script by Joanna Dickerson and Linda Morgan)

This storyboard managed to fool the censors – the nearest Beattie and
Harry will ever get to a bed scene. Rest assured, Harry has one foot on the
floor, if not both.

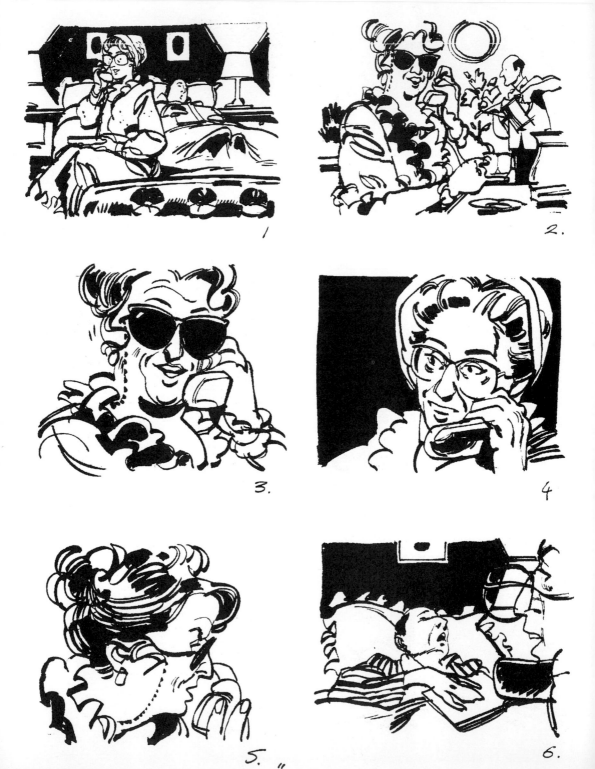

7.

8.

9.

10.

11.

12.

Somewhere in Willesden, insomnia reigns.

(Beattie thinks) He's asleep, I'm awake. It's too late to phone Hetty. Who in the world would be awake at this time for a chat? (Hums 'Waltzing Matilda' as she dials.)

Beattie: 'Hello, Rose? It's me, Beattie.'

Somewhere in Sydney – with a wonderful view but very little privacy – Rose is instantly alarmed by the sound of her sister's voice for no apparent reason . . .

Rose: 'Beattie?' (rising alarm) 'What's happened?'

(Beattie thinks) Straightaway she's hysterical! I blame all that sunshine and shark meat and no ozone layer . . .

Beattie: 'Nothing's happened.'

Rose hears the unmistakable tenor of strained nerves in her sister's blatant cover-up. She jumps, leaps even, to the conclusion that was obvious to everyone 30 years ago.

Rose: 'You can't fool me. It's Harry, isn't it? I may be 12,000 miles away but I'm still your sister. What is it: another woman?'

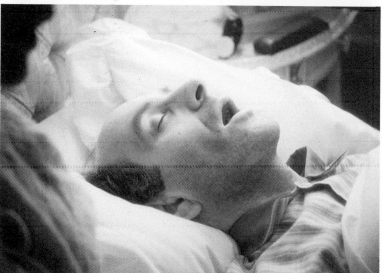

(Beattie thinks) She's been watching Neighbours *for too long. My Harry. Look at him. I'd like to meet the woman in question – she should have a gold medal for optimism . . .*

Beattie: 'Don't be . . .'

Beattie: '. . . ridiculous, Rose.'

Rose changes tack. If it's not the husband it has to be the son – the one they never said no to.

Rose (thinking on the bright side): 'So it's Melvyn? Melvyn's left Bernice? Oh, what a tragedy! The kids – one week with him, one week with her.'

Rose has known many such cases over the years and is prepared to list them – family by family – to help.

(Beattie thinks) In my family these things simply do not arise. Why? Because I brought them up.

Beattie: 'Melvyn and Bernice are fine.'

Rose can draw but one conclusion. It does not surprise her.

Rose: 'So it's Elaine.'

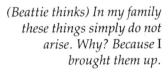

(Rose thinks) How many times has she told Cyril that Beattie's daughter was heading for TROUBLE with her beatnik ways, and wouldn't last long with the wallpaper salesman she finally married . . .

Rose: 'Elaine's left Raymond. I can't say I'm surprised. You know, your daughter is like her Aunty Rose – she needs space – send her out to me for a break.'

(Rose) There's a dentist divorcing his hygenist in . . .

(Beattie) Did I ring 12,000 miles for the ramblings of a sick woman?

Beattie: 'Harry is with me. Melvyn is with Bernice. Elaine is with Raymond.'

Rose: 'There's no special reason for phoning?'

Beattie: 'I just thought it would be nice to have a gossip.'

Rose is reluctant to believe in her sister's lack of ulterior motive. She's known her too many years.

Rose: 'So Harry is still with you, Melvyn is still with Bernice, Elaine is still with Raymond . . .'

Rose: '. . . this she calls gossip?'

(Rose thinks) And she used to be such fun!

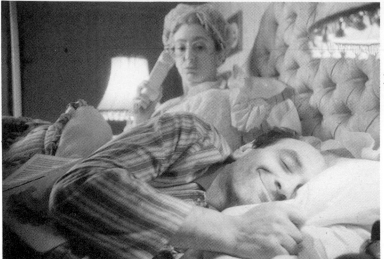

In his sleep, Harry dreams of his first bum-freezer mohair jacket and of the girl that went with it.

Harry: 'Oh, Beryl!'

Wide awake and waspish his wife catches his drift.

Beattie: 'Who's Beryl?'

(Beattie thinks) Beryl who? Could it be? Maybe Rose wasn't so wrong from 12,000 miles.

Beattie: 'Do you know a Beryl?'

Beattie: '... He's rolled over in his sleep and said "Beryl", I didn't know he had it in him.'

Is there a hint of grudging admiration? Is there life in the old dog yet?

I can't help feeling a bit weepy when I see this. My little grandson Oliver (what a little devil – already you should see him with the girls) singing Happy birthday to me. That's his mother, Melvyn's wife Bernice, holding the phone. The less said about her the better . . .

A snapshot: a shot of me that is, about to snap! If I ever get my hands on that Mrs Jones

My sister Rose in Sydney, Australia. Some people say we're alike but I can't see it myself.

Don't let the smile deceive you. Melvyn's late for dinner (the hours he has to work to pay for *her* expensive taste!) and I've got nothing to make him a sandwich with.

MRS BEATTIE'S RECIPES

HELEN'S KNAIDLACH

4 eggs
1 cup matzo meal

3 tablespoons chicken fat
1 teaspoon salt/pepper to taste

Method: Beat eggs until very light. Add other ingredients gradually. Form balls of size desired (should be firm so that they will not fall apart). Drop into boiling soup and cook for 15 mins.

SHEILA WOOLLEY'S EGG AND ONION

(Simple but eloquent. Amplex tablets obligatory afterwards for close personal contact.)

1 large Spanish onion
Salt and pepper

2 eggs

Method: Chop onion finely, and fry in butter for 15 mins (until very tender). Stir constantly. Drop in two eggs, salt and pepper and scramble well together.

THELMA GREEN'S LOKSHEN PUDDING

(Warning – reading this recipe puts on weight)

1 packet wide Lokshen
2 eggs
2 tablespoons custard

¼ lb butter
2 cups milk
1 pinch cinnamon

Method: After boiling lokshen soft in salt water, pour cold water over it and strain. Mix thoroughly with all other ingredients and then bake in a greased oven dish.

LOSE WEIGHT
THE BEATTIE WAY!

ZELMA'S CHOPPED LIVER
(Ox Liver or Chicken Liver mixed)

Fry two or three onions in oil or Tomar (if you can't get it where you live then move!) then when slightly brown, add slices of liver. Cook for about four minutes on either side, or until fairly soft. Hard boil three eggs. Mince liver, onions and eggs together (or chop – you can't beat an old fashioned chopper I always say), add a dash of salt and pepper, then blend together with melted Mazchick (if you can't get it where you live now then move again!), or chicken fat, rendered. I think melted Tomar can be used if nothing else.

RAE BLANK'S GEFILTE FISH
(boiled – Harry's favourite. I never make them much.)

2 lbs fish
1 egg
Salt and pepper
A pinch of cinnamon

2 large onions
½ teaspoon sugar
1 beetroot
1 carrot

Method: Salt and wash the fish. Skin, fillet and mince with one large onion. Add one egg, pepper, sugar, cinnamon, breadcrumbs and water. Mix well. Put bones and head in a saucepan with sliced onions, carrot, beetroot. Make fish mixture into balls and place in saucepan on top of bones, and cover well with water. Allow to cook gently for two hours, adding more water if necessary.

Melvyn's Promotion

A Worried Woman

The Driving Test

Guess Who's Coming
to Dinner?

Melvyn's Promotion

(Harry thinks) If she's going to phone Australia, I'm going to eat the last of the smoked salmon!

(Beattie) I'll be lucky to find her in at this time – she'll be sipping Margaritas at the bridge club – ha! Oh wait – she's in.

Beattie: 'Hello, Rose, it's Beattie. I had to call. Melvyn's been promoted.'

Rose: 'Promoted!'

Rose: 'Oh Beattie, that's marvellous news!'

(Rose) I must let Cyril hear this – he's never had a good word to say for my sister's eldest.

Rose: 'Little Melvyn, promoted.'

(Rose) I can't remember what field he was in.

Rose: 'What's he been promoted to, Beattie?'

(Beattie) Now, I must get this right . . . I sometimes get confused myself . . .

Beattie: 'Well, you know he was Acting Assistant Deputy Sales Executive.'

(Rose) These English titles kill me!

Rose: 'Executive – get her!'

Beattie: 'And now he doesn't have to act any more. Now he's the genuine Assistant Deputy Sales Executive.'

Melvyn's Promotion

(Rose) Well, he always was a plodder, but at least he's plodding upwards.

Rose: 'Oh, Beattie, that's wonderful news, it really is ...'

(Beattie) I knew she'd be pleased. It's worth a call. Keeping the family informed.

Rose: 'When you think of what he was like when he was a little boy ...'

(Rose) A real wingeing pom. She had him in nappies till he was four. And food – could that child eat! The last time I saw him he had to come sideways through the patio doors!

Rose: 'Who would have imagined little Melvyn would do so well? I can't believe it, I really can't.'

(Beattie) She can't believe it! She ca . . . What does she mean she can't believe it? Why can't she believe it?

Beattie (frostily): Why?

Rose: 'Why what?'

(Beattie) Hello. It's started. The veiled insult in the voice. Nothing's ever good enough, is it? Nothing travels like envy.

Beattie: 'Why can't you believe it?'

Melvyn's Promotion

(Beattie) If she's going to start – I'll have to finish it. Her children, I suppose, are paragons!

Beattie: 'You think there was something wrong with Melvyn when he was a little boy? All these years ...'

Beattie: '... you've never said anything. Now, now it comes out ...'

(Beattie) Her son – the beach bum with his tochas hanging out of his behamas. And the daughter who's had her nose altered so many times she looks like Jack Pallance – oh, they're perfect – but my Melvyn ...

MARY CAPLAN'S FUZNOGGY
(not *the same thing as you used to do at parties. Not me of course* . . .)

1 knuckle bone
1 lb shin
Salt, pepper to taste

3–4 eggs
1 clove garlic

Method: Put all ingredients in a pressure cooker, fill with water, pressure cook for 2½–3 hours. Hard boil 3–4 eggs. Mince the cooked shin, and put a thick layer in a large pyrex dish. Slice the hard boiled eggs and place on top of the meat. Cool the liquid, strain, and pour over eggs and minnced shin. Leave to set. Remove fat when cold.

LILY LANG'S EGGPLANT CUTLETS
(*Aubergine – I never like the look of an aubergine until I've got its skin off. I don't know why . . .*)

1 egg-plant
3 eggs
1 grated onion
½ teaspoon salt
¼ teaspoon pepper

1 ½ cups of matzo meal
2 cups stewed tomatoes
3 tablespoons of sugar
juice of ½ lemon

Method: Bake whole egg-plant until soft, remove skin and mash well. Mix in beaten eggs, onion, salt and pepper and meal. Form small cakes, brown them in hot fat, then place in baking pan. Season tomatoes with lemon and sugar, pour over the cutlets and bake in moderate oven for ½ hour. Serve hot or cold.

A Worried Woman

Beattie, who was born in a trunk call, decides to call her brother in Canada.

Beattie: 'Hello? Lionel? It's Beattie.'

Somewhere in Canada we find Lionel, about to enjoy some barbecued mooseburgers.

Lionel (Surprised and pleased): 'Beattie? Well, how are you?'

(Beattie thinks) I mustn't show any concern in my voice that I haven't heard from him.

Beattie: 'I'm worried.'

Suddenly Lionel feels eight-years-old again and it's not a feeling he likes to feel.

Lionel: 'You're worried? What about?'

(Beattie) What does he think I'm worried about? Mrs Gorbachev?

Beattie: 'I'm worried about you.'

(Lionel) She's heard something that I haven't.

Lionel: 'You're worried about me? Why would you worry about me?'

(Beattie) He wants a reason. Six weeks passes in total silence and I'm supposed to be dancing and throwing cocktail parties.

Beattie: 'I'm worried about you because I worry about you.'

Lionel (trying to work this out):'You're worried about me because you worry about me?'

(Beattie) If he keeps repeating what I've just said, when I've made the phone call – I'll have to pretend we've been cut off.

Beattie: 'Well of course I worry about you.'

(Lionel) I'm in a time-warp – please God or an operator – cut this woman off.

(Beattie) It's the cold weather in Canada – it's closed his mind . . .

Beattie: 'You may have been in the middle of nowhere for the last 30 years . . .'

(Lionel) Already she's started with her maple leaf massacring . . .

Lionel: 'Toronto is not in the middle of nowhere.'

(Beattie) When our mother, God rest her soul, passed on, she left me to do the worrying for the whole family. It's a burden I've had to shoulder.

Beattie: 'Wherever, you're still my little brother.'

(Lionel) Sometimes she sounds just like my mother, God rest her soul.

Lionel (lump in throat): 'I'm still her little brother ...'

(Lionel) I could kill her!

(Lionel) Still – when I hear that whining long distance I miss her – I really do.

Lionel: '... still her little brother. Listen Beattie, I'm a big boy now. You don't have to worry.'

(Beattie) What does he mean? The elder sister – just – what else should I do?

Beattie: 'I don't have to worry?'

(Lionel) I'll just reassure her.

Lionel: 'Everything is OK.'

(Beattie) This is enthusiasm?

Beattie: 'Just OK.'

(Lionel) I'll re-reassure her.

Lionel: 'Everything is just fine.'

(Beattie) He's hedging – he's keeping something from me. I can tell by his voice.

Beattie: 'But only *just* fine.'

(Lionel) What does she want, a written affidavit?

Lionel: 'Everything is perfect!'

(Beattie) That's it. He's said it. He's tempted providence. This call was destiny. This man is depressed.

Beattie: 'Now I *am* worried. Lionel, when everything is perfect, it can only get worse.'

Beattie: '... Put it another way ...'

(Beattie) Thank God I rang in time to cheer him up!

Beattie: '... Every silver lining has a cloud.'

Beattie is parcelling. The parcel contains useful gifts for someone who has just passed his driving test. It is for her grandson, Anthony. His driving test is not until the following day, but to Beattie it is a foregone conclusion . . .

Beattie: 'Anthony? I just called to wish you luck.'

Anthony has been staring at the same page for several hours. For some reason nothing will go in. A not unfamiliar syndrome for Anthony . . .

Anthony: 'I'll need it.'

Beattie is on home ground. Reassurance is her middle name – insider information is her game.

Beattie: 'Nonsense! It's just a matter of making the right impression.'

If his grandmother would put the phone down he might conceivably get this ruddy page into his head . . . then start on page 2 . . .

Anthony: 'It's just a matter of remembering the whole of the highway code.'

(Beattie thinks) Bless him! The boy doesn't have a calculating bone in his brain. I'll explain to him about priorities – his mother should have done it, but if she's too busy with her aerobits . . .

Beattie: 'Never mind that, just remember to open the examiner's door.'

Anthony can't believe what he's hearing, until he remembers it's his grandma he's hearing it from . . .

Anthony: 'Open his door?'

The Driving Test

Beattie: 'When he goes to get in, open his door. Creates a marvellous impression opening a door. Something like that can make all the difference. It can open doors. And another thing, clean your shoes.'

Anthony: 'Clean my shoes?'

Anthony knows he is behaving like a trained parakeet, but he feels he has to repeat his grandmother's words in order to check both their sanities.

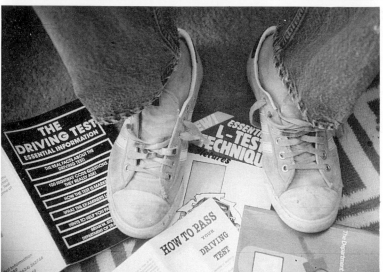

Beattie: 'They'll look nice against the pedals.'

This is a thing which the cognoscenti know from birth. Other, less fortunate people, need it explained to them (along with a definition of the word cognoscenti. You think I didn't read Mario Puzo? It was serialized in Woman's Weekly wasn't it?

(Beattie thinks) And now the piece of resistance! This has never been known to fail!

Beattie: 'If you really want to impress him, bring him round here. Show him what sort of family you come from. We'll have a cup of tea and a coconut macaroon.'

Anthony: 'Grandma, *I* don't decide where to drive, he *tells* me where to go.'

Beattie: 'So? You're going to lose marks for showing a bit of initiative?'

(Beattie thinks) This child has no confidence, no belief in himself. I don't say it's entirely the mother's fault, but where else could he not get it from . . .?

Beattie: 'Honestly, I don't know who he takes after . . .'

Harry appears at the door grappling with the complexities of a plastic watering can.

Beattie: '. . . Yes I do!'

(Beattie thinks) Still, thank God he's got my looks . . .

In the beginning there was a storyboard: A quiet Thursday in Willesden.
Dark has fallen. A doorbell rings, and the nightmare begins . . .

10 11. 12

13 14 15

16 17 18

Guess Who's Coming to Dinner?

Dolly and Gerald have braved a cold evening (and a row over having to stop at a confectioner's shop so as not to appear at the door empty-handed) in order to arrive at their old friends Beattie and Harry's for a dinner engagement.

Dolly: 'Sorry we're late.'

Beattie, having just given Harry his fishfingers in the kitchen, is amazed but not displeased to see her friends. They've obviously popped in for a coffee on their way back from somewhere. A phonecall first wouldn't have hurt. So she could have taken off her pinny and put on her rouge. But listen, what are friends for if you can't be yourself with them?

Gerald: Hope we haven't spoilt the dinner.'

(Beattie thinks) Late? Dinner? Chocolates she's given me? What does he mean dinner? Has the whole world gone mad? Am I dreaming? Is it a nightmare – like in Dallas?

Gerald: 'Where's old Harry boy then?'

Gerald is not an abstemious man. He has been hungry for 2 hours. He was hungry when he came in from work; hungry when he watched his wife dress up for her evening out; hungry all the way over and he can't smell food! (Certainly not a proper dinner smell.) The sooner he sees the fourth member of the party, the sooner they'll eat!

Beattie: 'Harry? Oh, he's just uncorking the sherry. Won't be a mo ...'

(Beattie thinks) I'll have to stall them! Oh my God! My heart! What have I got in? A tin of pink salmon – between four of us? Oy, Harry's just eaten – he'll have to eat again! Eat what though? I've got to think! How long do baked potatoes take in a microwave? I haven't got a microwave! I'm going mad! Harry'll think of something ...

Beattie: 'It's Dolly and Gerald. They've come for dinner!'

Harry: 'Come for dinner?!'

Beattie: 'I could have sworn I said Thursday!'

(Beattie) This is the worst moment of my life, since my sister was evacuated and I wasn't. Think Harry, think! What am I saying? What's he going to think, even if he thinks? Look at him. No help.
I'll never be able to look them in the face again. I'll be a laughing stock. Wait ... I've got it. Severe illness ...

Beattie: 'There's only one thing for it. You'll have to have one of your turns.'

Harry: 'Turns? What turns?'

Harry has been disoriented and deprived of oxygen, and he doesn't know why.

Meanwhile, in the lounge . . .

Dolly: 'I could have sworn she said Tuesday.'

Gerald: 'Well, what are we going to do? I'm starving!'

Something is horribly amiss and it means that Dolly is embarrassed and Gerald is convinced he'll never eat again.

Dolly: 'Only one thing for it. You'll have to have one of your turns.'

Gerald is now confused, starving and unable to breathe.

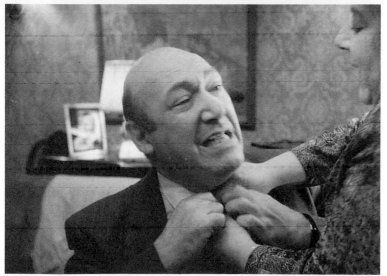

Gerald: 'Turns? What turns?'

(Gerald thinks) If I do a turn will they feed me?

Beattie and Dolly (accidentally in unison): 'I'm afraid you'll have to excuse us ... It's Harry/Gerald ... He's having one of his turns!'

Gerald: 'She could still make me a sandwich!'

Here's that Maureen Lipton person in rehearsal. (I wouldn't want to be an actor, it's always hand to mouth.)

I *always* insist on having a well-read sound crew.

My home, which has variously been at Wembley, Shepperton and Elstree. Can't imagine what Prince Charles would make of this architecture!

My sister Rose and her husband Cyril (Clive Swift in one of his most arduous roles) sitting it out while Richard takes issue with the Vegemite.

The prop man trying to decorate my table with a wedding present we got from Harry's sister, Mabel. She never did have much taste.

Brian 'Buddy' Greene and Sandra Caron, alias Lionel and Norma, my brother and sister-in-law in Toronto.

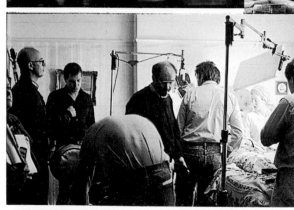

What I have to put up with in my own bedroom!

Geoffrey Chiswick, Bernard Bresslaw and Miriam Margoyles (back to the camera – she's very shy), aka Harry, Gerald and Dolly, discussing 'action' with me, Eddie Collins, (the camera operator – the one with the lovely hair), Frazer Copp, first assistant director, and Richard Phillips (the one whose hair we don't mention).

AWARDS WON BY BRITISH TELECOM IN 1988

BRITISH TELEVISION
ADVERTISING AWARDS

SILVER
Not Keeping Up With the
Joneses, Anthony and the
Ology (*Corporate*)
Melvyn (the Telephobic Son),
Something for Nothing, A
Voice Like an Angel!, *Not*
Keeping up with the Joneses,
Anthony and the Ology, The
Answerphone (*Campaign*)
BRONZE
Melvyn (the Telephobic Son),
A Voice Like an Angel!,
(*Corporate*)
DIPLOMA
Something for Nothing
(Corporate)

NEW YORK ART
DIRECTORS CLUB
GOLD
Anthony and the Ology, A
Voice Like an Angel!, *Not*
Keeping Up with the Joneses
(*Campaign*)

CREATIVE CIRCLE
HONOURS
GOLD
Anthony and the Ology, A
Voice Like an Angel!,
Something for Nothing (*Best
Use of Humour*)
SILVER
Melvyn (the Telephobic Son)
(*Best Use of Personality*)
BRONZE
A Voice Like an Angel! (*Best
TV Script*)

CANNES ADVERTISING
FILM FESTIVAL
GOLD
Not Keeping Up with the
Joneses, A Voice Like an
Angel!, The Answerphone
(*Campaign*)

CAMPAIGN MAGAZINE
Campaign of the Year 1988

TV TIMES
Readers' Favourite Campaign
1988

CLIO
Best Campaign 1988

AWARDS WON BY BRITISH
TELECOM IN 1989

D&AD (Accepted for
publication in 1989 Annual)
The Call That Never Came,
The Dangling Fiancée, Do You
Have a 12 in the Green?
(*Campaign*)
The Dangling Fiancée, Do You
Have a 12 in the Green? (*Up to
60 seconds*)

CREATIVE CIRCLE AWARDS
GOLD
Do You Have a 12 in the
Green? (*Best use of humour*)
The Dangling Fiancée (*Best use
of dialogue*)
BRONZE
Do You Have a 12 in the
Green? The Call that Never
Came, Melvyn (the
Workaholic Son), We'll Meet
Again (*Campaign*)

BRITISH TELEVISION
AWARDS
SILVER
We'll Meet Again, Melvyn (the
Workaholic Son), The Call
That Never Came, Do You
Have a 12 in the Green?
(*Campaign*)

GOLDEN BREAK AWARDS
**BEST COMEDY
PERFORMANCE**
Do You Have a 12 in the
Green?

BEST ACTRESS
The Dangling Fiancée

THE ONE SHOW NEW YORK
SILVER
Do You Have a 12 in the
Green?

MARKETING WEEK
Award for Creative Excellence
– **GOLD**

CANNES ADVERTISING
FILM FESTIVAL

GOLD CAMPAIGN AWARD

OLIVE'S GRIMSLICH

Two matzos
2 oz fine meal
2 oz ground almonds
2 tablespoons melted fat

2 eggs
4 oz dried fruit
½ teaspoon cinnamon
2 oz sugar

Method: Soak up matzo in cold water till soft, then squeeze very dry and beat up with a fork. Separate yolks and whites of the eggs, add the beaten yolks and remaining ingredients. Mix well, then fold in stiffly whipped egg whites. Drop in spoonfuls in hot shallow fat and fry until golden brown on both sides. (What did people do before the invention of the frying pan?) Sprinkle with sugar.

ENA PHILLIPS'S POTATO LATKES
(without which no dinner is a meal)

6 raw potatoes
2 eggs
2 tablespoons matzo meal

1 large onion
1 tablespoon self raising flour
Salt and pepper

Method: Grate potato (taking the skin off your fingers every time – if some goes in it won't harm) and drain off the water. Add the grated onion, eggs, flour, matzo meal and seasoning. Mix very well. Drop tablespoons of mixture into boiling deep oil. Turn until both sides are golden brown. Drain well.